# BADASS SURVIVAL SECRETS

# BADASS SURVIVAL SECRETS

### Essential Skills to Survive Any Crisis

**JAMES HENRY**

Skyhorse Publishing

Skyhorse Publishing books may be purchased in bulk at special discounts for sales promotion, corporate gifts, fund-raising, or educational purposes. Special editions can also be created to specifications. For details, contact the Special Sales Department, Skyhorse Publishing, 307 West 36th Street, 11th Floor, New York, NY 10018 or info@skyhorsepublishing.com.

Please visit our website at www.skyhorsepublishing.com

10 9 8 7 6 5 4 3 2

Library of Congress Cataloging-in-Publication Data is available on file.

Cover design by Jane Sheppard

Print ISBN: 978-1-62914-733-8
Ebook ISBN: 978-1-62914-864-9

Printed in the United States of America

# TABLE OF CONTENTS

## CHAPTER 1

# SURVIVAL IS USUALLY AN UNPLANNED NIGHT IN THE WOODS

Each year dozens of American outdoor enthusiasts find themselves in an unexpected outdoor emergency. They get lost, injured, or stranded and suddenly find themselves depending upon survival skills to survive. For most people, thanks to modern communications such as cell phones and two-way radios, it is merely a sobering two- or three-hour adventure. In fact, with today's methods of search and rescue, the majority of missing people are found within 72 hours after they have been reported missing, most even less. However, for some who do not take the proper precautions or do not have survival skills, such an experience can end in tragedy.

The purpose of this book is to help you prepare for that "unplanned night or nights in the woods." Keep it with you to help you make it through the adventure. With proper preparation for any outdoor activity, there should be little reason for an unplanned night in the woods. But, should you find yourself in a situation where you will need to survive several days, this book will have you prepared to do it with style. Survival knowledge and training pays off when the chips are down. Remember the acronym, "LOST"—Lean On Survival Training.

North America still has lots of back-country in which it is easy to get lost or stranded. Even in the most remote country, however, most missing people are found within a few hours.

## SURVIVAL TRAINING PAYS

Several years ago, when I was working as a wildlife manager in Georgia, I helped lead the search for a missing hunter in the rugged mountains along the Georgia–North Carolina boundary. We were told that this hunter had little hunting experience but had received extensive survival training. In a blinding rainstorm, it

A sudden spill in a canoe can leave you stranded.

took us two days to find the lost hunter. Much to our surprise, by the time we found him he had virtually established a comfortable homestead.

When he first realized he was lost, he stopped walking and picked an opening in the dense woods to establish a survival camp. He immediately put out ground-to-air signals. Realizing bad weather was on the way, he built a shelter under some overhanging rocks that kept him dry and out of the wind. He gathered plenty of firewood and stored it in his shelter. Next, he built a fire complete with a reflector to keep his shelter warm.

It was his fire that led to his being found. The hunter's survival camp was so comfortable that those of us in the search party used it for an overnight rest before packing out.

**When you first realize you are lost, stop. Do not wander around aimlessly. For every hour you wander the search area grows four times.**

Due to his survival training, he lived comfortably through a two-day storm. He stayed positive and worked toward being found. He used the resources at hand to make a survival camp. Will you be like this hunter if your time comes to spend an unplanned night or two in the woods?

# HOW TO USE THIS LITTLE BOOK

1. When you first get this book, sit down and **READ it**. Think about what you are reading and how it can apply to you and your outings.

2. Reread the chapter entitled **"Survival Kits"** and make a list of the items you need to purchase to put one together.

3. On a weekend you want to do something that is fun and educational, take your survival kit into the woods and spend the night using the items in the kit. Upon completion of the **overnight test**, be sure to replace any items that may be difficult to repack into a compact package. This exercise may also help you discover items you will want in your survival kit that my list did not include. Remember it is YOUR survival kit, so modify it to meet your needs.

4. **This book covers only the most basic navigational skills.** I feel this requires training that, like first aid, you should have before you start exploring the backcountry. If you haven't had training in the proper use of your GPS or map and compass, get it ASAP. That alone can keep you from ever needing this book.

5. **This book covers only the most basic first-aid skills.** It is my belief that everyone who ventures into the backcountry should have successfully taken a Red Cross first-aid course. Also, those who have special medical conditions should be skilled in managing them.

6. **Place this book in your survival kit** so it will be there if, and when, you need it to guide you through a survival situation. It was designed to be small enough to fit into your kit, and concise enough to be a quick and easy resource when you are in trouble.

7. If you find yourself in a lost or stranded situation, **stop, sit down, think, remain calm, don't panic, and plan to stay put.**

By gaining control of yourself in these first few minutes, you have increased your chances of survival by 50 percent.

8. When you first realize you are lost and in trouble is the time to dig this book out and use it to guide you toward a safe wait until you are found.

9. As a Maine game warden once said, "Even in today's modern world there are many trappers and guides that spend the night in the woods with little more than what is found in a basic survival kit, they spend their lives doing it. Relax—you may even enjoy your unplanned stay in the woods."

Take a first-aid course and keep your training up-to-date. You may have to treat your own injuries in a survival emergency.

## CHAPTER 2

# SEARCH & RESCUE

## MODERN SEARCH & RESCUE WORKS FOR YOU

If you have taken the time and precaution to file a trip plan with a responsible person before your outing, then should you not return on time, you will not go unnoticed for very long. This will begin a series of events that will result in your being rescued quickly.

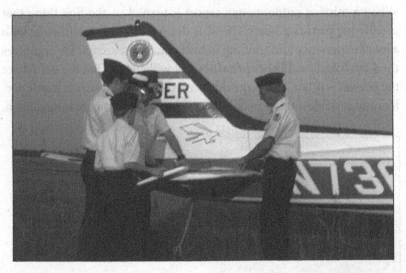

Many missing people give up hope quickly because they think no one is looking for them. Modern search and rescue is usually on the site within a few hours.

One of the most common, and dangerous, fears most lost or stranded people have is that no one will know to come looking for them. If you have followed the steps in the next chapter of this book, then you can put this fear to rest; trained people will be looking for you soon. If you stay put once you realize you are lost, then it will take even less time to find you. Trying to walk out, panicking and running will work against you; and it will take much longer for rescuers to find you. For every hour a lost person walks, the search area grows four times larger. You should stay put and wait to be found!

## HERE IS HOW IT WORKS.

A search starts quickly when you are reported missing to local authorities. In most cases, this is the county sheriff, district forest ranger or conservation officer. In Canada it is usually the Royal Canadian Mounted Police. Today, many of these officers have received formal training in search and rescue organization and know how to respond quickly to a missing outdoorsman emergency.

When a missing outdoorsman report is turned in, the first thing that usually happens is a "search boss" is designated. This is someone with a lot of experience and training in backcountry searches. He organizes the search and establishes priorities. He will ensure that the site where the person was last seen is quickly protected, set up a search headquarters and interview those people who were last with the missing person.

The search director will quickly establish the "area of probability" and the search will be centered there.

Protecting the "last seen" area keeps wellmeaning people from destroying tracks and other important signs expert trackers will need for tracking the lost person.

The interview with the missing person's friends/family is most important, as this is where the search boss learns much about the missing person. If a trip plan has been left with someone, it will cut down on the time it takes to get an organized search started. They will have a good idea where to begin looking.

Early in the search, specially trained dogs may be used to trail the missing person. Two to four aircraft are used to quickly locate missing outdoorsmen.

The interviewer will be looking for detailed information on the missing person. The person's name, address, description, clothing worn, boot type (sole information is important to trackers), age, equipment he has with him, medical conditions including medications, experience in the outdoors, physical condition, personality traits, etc. All of this information is important to experienced searchers because it tells them a lot about where to look for the missing person.

Usually the first searchers to hit the trail include trackers with dogs and a hasty team. The hasty team is made up of highly specialized people who go into the most likely areas the missing person is believed to be. This is why it is important to stay put when you first realize you are lost.

At the same time, lookouts and road check teams are posted. Lookouts are located at observation points in the search area and road search teams ride roads near the search area looking for the missing person.

As quickly as possible, aircraft will be brought into the search; often aircraft with specialized equipment to electronically help find the missing person. At that point, the search boss may set up grid searches supervised by professionals and carried out using volunteers.

Many people who are lost fear searchers will only look a few hours then give up, thinking the missing person is dead. This is not true. Most search bosses estimate how long the missing person can survive under the conditions and then plan to search three times that long, if needed. Search efforts go far beyond reasonable expectations.

Lost and stranded people should never give up hope. The search will go on until you are rescued. How fast that search begins, however, depends upon how well you prepared before you went into the woods!

Aircraft are used to quickly locate missing outdoorsmen.

## CHAPTER 3

# BASIC SURVIVAL TIPS

"If hope is out there, hope can get you through."

*—NASA Astronaut Jerry Linenger, who spent months stranded on the Russian Space Station*

## MAIN TIPS TO REMEMBER

### THE ONLY PERSON YOU CAN ULTIMATELY COUNT ON IS YOURSELF.

No one else can give you the mental will, physical stamina, and common sense that you're going to need to survive. So don't depend on others—you may be alone! Make your plans, pack your own survival kit, and if something unplanned happens when you are on your own in the wild, be prepared to take care of your own needs as well as the needs of your teammates.

This self-sufficient attitude is empowering in itself. Remember that your life depends on what you do, not on the chance that a teammate will be there to do for you what you can't do for yourself.

### ALWAYS LEAVE BEHIND DETAILED PLANS AND TIMETABLES WITH A TRUSTED PERSON.

That way, if you're missing, a search party is likely to be sent out sooner than later if you fail to arrive back when expected.

## PREPARE FOR THE SIX CONTINGENCIES.

1. Becoming lost. It's not enough to rely on your good sense of direction. Always carry at least one compass, a map, and GPS and a SPOT or locating device.
2. Darkness. With darkness we shift from relying primarily on seeing to relying primarily on hearing. This is an uncomfortable change for some people. Remember that darkness can be your friend. Treat it with respect, and don't move into areas where you could get hurt by your inability to see.
3. Being stranded. There are countless contingencies under which you could be stuck in the wilderness for an extended period of time. Anticipate that this could happen and plan for ways to alert others and make your way to safety.
4. Illness or injury. Any time you go into the wilderness, there's always the possibility that you can become injured or ill. Practice and develop your own wilderness first-aid skills.
5. Extreme weather. There is no such thing as bad weather, just different types of weather. Always be prepared. Snow, rain, or extreme heat or cold can impact your ability to survive. Before heading out, make sure you have the proper clothing, water, and the ability to shelter yourself for extended periods of time.

## IF LOST, STOP AND DO A MAP STUDY.

Don't move unless you know where you are and where you are going. Many very experienced point men and navigators have become lost or disoriented in the wild. Remember that the consequences of panic can be fatal. Take a break, do a good map study, reevaluate your situation, and allow the adrenaline that has flooded your system and put you in fight or flight mode to subside.

## ASSESS YOUR SITUATION AS OBJECTIVELY AS YOU CAN.

1. Treat any injuries—yours or your teammates. Self aid and buddy aid. Your health is most important for survival.
2. What needs to be done to assure your safety? Do you need to move to a safer area?

3. Observe the area of your location. What are the hazards? Are there enemy or friendly forces in the immediate area? What are the advantages? Is there water nearby? What can you take advantage of to help you survive?
4. Plan your next move carefully. Work out a plan in your head first. If you're satisfied with it, proceed. If not, give yourself time to come up with a better alternative.

## TAKE STOCK OF YOUR SUPPLIES AND IMMEDIATE NEEDS.

A healthy man can survive for several weeks without food and several days without water. So water is your most important requirement. Under normal circumstances, the human body requires two quarts of water daily to maintain adequate hydration.

Don't ration the water you have to last for many days. Drink what you need. It's better to have water in your body than in a bottle or canteen. Conserve water lost through sweating by wearing a hat, sitting in the shade, moving only at night, and so on.

In most terrain, you will eventually find water when moving downhill. Watch animals, or follow their tracks. They'll usually lead to water. Birds tend to congregate near water, too. Remember that water from streams and ponds should be boiled before drinking or purified by other means—tablets, straw, filter, boiling, etc.

Maps

**13**

## SIGNAL.

Always carry a whistle, mirror, and matches to start a fire. Smoke is visible from far away in the day.

## FIND FOOD.

Food isn't an immediate concern unless you're reasonably sure that rescue is many days or weeks off. As a general rule, avoid plant life unless you know for a fact that something is edible. If it walks, swims, flies, slithers, or crawls, it's probably

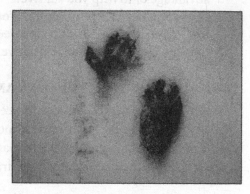

**Raccoon footprints**

safe to eat. All fur-bearing animals are edible. All birds are edible. Grubs found in rotten logs are edible, as are almost all insects.

## FIRE REQUIRES THREE ELEMENTS:

Oxygen, fuel, and a source of heat. Is your fuel thin and dry enough? Is your heat source hot enough to light the tinder? Is there enough oxygen reaching the point where the heat meets the fuel? Identify the problem and proceed.

# SURVIVAL IS THE ABILITY AND THE DESIRE TO STAY ALIVE, SOMETIMES ALONE AND UNDER ADVERSE CIRCUMSTANCES.

Understand and master each part of this definition.

1. Ability. Be proficient at building shelter, starting a fire, signaling for help, and staying hydrated.
2. Desire. Regardless of how bad the situation might be, never lose the will to survive and always maintain a positive attitude.
3. Stay alive. Your ability to effectively deal with life-threatening medical situations is of the highest priority. Stay current with your emergency medical skills.

4. Under adverse conditions. The more you know about your environment ahead of time, the greater your advantage.
5. Alone. Never count on the help of others. Be self-proficient since you may end up alone.
6. Until rescued, be patient. It's your job to keep yourself and your teammates alive.

# LEARN TO DEAL WITH THE ENEMIES OF SURVIVAL:

1. Pain
2. Cold and/or Heat
3. Thirst
4. Hunger
5. Fatigue

### THE RULE OF THREES

A human being can survive:

- three minutes without air
- three hours without a regulated body temperature
- three days without water
- three weeks without food

**In summary, here is a list of common-sense survival tips:**

1. Always carry a map, at least one compass, a GPS and a SPOT or something similar.
2. Dress using layers to avoid overheating.
3. Carry water and water purification tablets or filter when possible. During the map studies, always identify alternate water sources.

Compass

4. Carry high-calorie energy food such as protein bars in your second and third line gear.

# THE CASE OF ARON RALSTON

Can you imagine amputating your arm with a blunt knife? As excruciatingly painful and inconceivable as it sounds, that turned out to be the only option left to 28-year-old Aron Ralston after an 800-pound boulder fell on his arm, pinning it to a canyon wall.

From midday Saturday, April 26, 2003, until midday Thursday, May 1, Ralston was stuck in a remote area of Canyonlands National Park in Utah alone and unable to free himself. He had little food and water. No one would even wonder where he was until he didn't show up for work on Tuesday. Unable to sit, lie down, use his right arm, or sleep, he knew that he was in for an excruciatingly difficult time. Those 120 hours of what he calls "uninterrupted experience" tested to the fullest his physical, mental, emotional, and spiritual being.

Finally, on May 1, 2003, he did the unthinkable, first using the boulder to leverage his arm until the bones snapped and then sawing away at muscle and tendon with his pocketknife. He then rappelled down a sixty-five-foot wall and was later found by hikers as he walked back to his car.

He survived, wrote a best-selling book about his experience (*Between a Rock and a Hard Place*), and continues to climb. He later admitted that his big mistake was not telling anyone where he was going.

**Canyonlands National Park, Utah**

## CHAPTER 4

# NAVIGATION

Assess the threat and apply appropriate evasion principles.

**1. Stay or Move Considerations**
  a.  Stay with the vehicle/aircraft in a non-combat environment.
  b.  Leave only when—
    (1)  Dictated by the threat.
    (2)  Are certain of your location, have a known destination, and have the ability to get there.
    (3)  Can reach water, food, shelter, and/or help.
    (4)  Convinced rescue is not coming.
  c.  Consider the following if you decide to travel:
    (1)  Follow the briefed evasion plan.
    (2)  Determine which direction to travel and why.
    (3)  Decide what equipment to take, cache, or destroy.
  d.  Leave information at your starting point (in a non-combat environment) that includes—
    (1)  Destination.
    (2)  Route of travel.
    (3)  Personal condition.
    (4)  Supplies available.
  e.  Consider the following for maps (in a combat environment):
    (1)  *DO NOT* write on the map.
    (2)  *DO NOT* soil the map by touching the destination.
    (3)  *DO NOT* fold in a manner providing travel information.

Note: *These actions may compromise information if captured.*

## 2. Navigation and Position Determination

a.  Determine your general location by—
   (1) Developing a working knowledge of the operational area.
      (a) Geographic checkpoints.
      (b) Man-made checkpoints.
      (c) Previous knowledge of operational area.
   (2) Using the *Rate x Time = Distance* formula.
   (3) Using information provided in the map legend.
   (4) Using prominent landmarks.
   (5) Visualizing map to determine position.
b.  Determine cardinal directions (north, south, east, and west) by—
   (1) Using compass.

**CAUTION:** The following methods are *NOT* highly accurate and give only general cardinal direction.

   (2) Using stick and shadow method to determine a true north-south line.

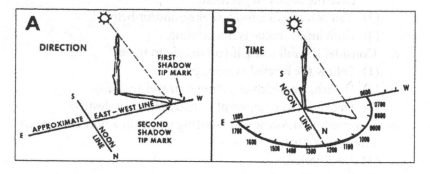

**Stick and Shadow Method**

   (3) Remembering the sunrise/moonrise is in the east and sunset/moonset is in the west.
   (4) Using a wristwatch to determine general cardinal direction.

(a) Digital watches. Visualize a clock face on the watch.
(b) Northern Hemisphere. Point hour hand at the sun. South is halfway between the hour hand and 12 o'clock position.
(c) Southern Hemisphere. Point the 12 o'clock position on your watch at the sun. North is halfway between the 12 o' clock position and the hour hand.

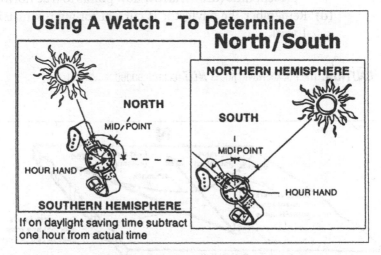

## Using A Watch - To Determine North/South

NORTHERN HEMISPHERE

NORTH

MID / POINT

HOUR HAND

SOUTHERN HEMISPHERE

If on daylight saving time subtract one hour from actual time

SOUTH

MIDI POINT

HOUR HAND

**Direction Using a Watch**

(5) Using a pocket navigator—
(a) Gather the following necessary materials:
- Flat writing material (such as an MRE box).
- 1–2 inch shadow tip device (a twig, nail, or match).
- Pen or pencil.
(b) Start construction at sunup; end construction at sundown. Do the following:
- Attach shadow tip device in center of paper.
- Secure navigator on flat surface (*DO NOT* move during set up period).
- Mark tip of shadow every 30 minutes annotating the time.
- Connect marks to form an arc.
- Indicate north with a drawn arrow.

**Note**: The shortest line between base of shadow tip device and curved line is a north-south line.

      (c)  Do the following during travel:
- Hold navigator so the shadow aligns with mark of present time (drawn arrow now points to true north).

      (d)  Remember the navigator is current tor approximately 1 week.

**CAUTION:** The Pocket Navigator is **NOT** recommended if evading.

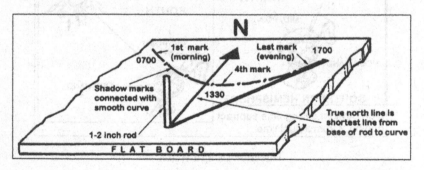

**Pocket Navigator**

(6)  Using the stars the—
      (a)  North Star is used to locate true north–south line.
      (b)  Southern Cross is used to locate true south–north line.

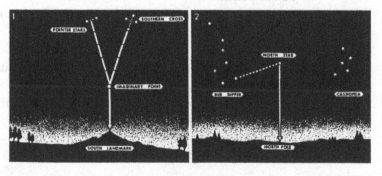

**Stars**

c. Orient the map by—
  (1) Using a true north–south line—
    (a) Unfold map and place on a firm, flat, level nonmetallic surface.
    (b) Align the compass on a true north–south line.
    (c) Rotate map and compass until stationary index line aligns with the magnetic variation indicated in marginal information.
      • Easterly (subtract variation from 360 degrees).
      • Westerly (add variation to 360 degrees).

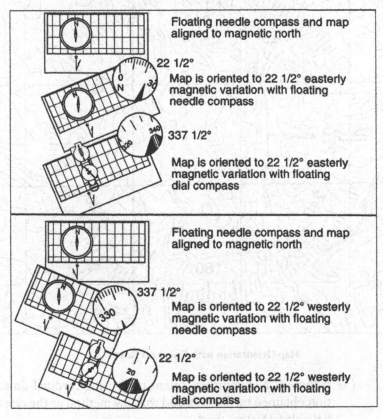

**Orienting a Map Using a True North–South Line**

  (2) Using a compass rose—
    (a) Place edge of the lensatic compass on magnetic north line of the compass rose closest to your location.

**21**

(b) Rotate map and compass until compass reads 360 degrees.

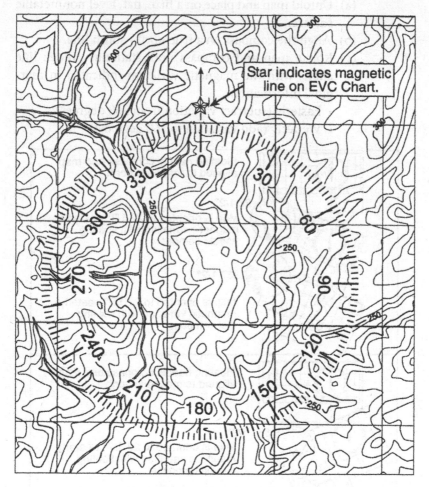

**Map Orientation with Compass Rose**

(3) If there is **NO** compass, orient map using cardinal direction obtained by the stick and shadow method or the celestial aids (stars) method.

d. Determine specific location.

(1) Global Positioning System (GPS).

(a) *DO NOT* use GPS for primary navigation.

(b) Use GPS to confirm your position *ONLY*.

(c) Select area providing maximum satellite reception.

(d) Conserve GPS battery life.

(2) Triangulation (resection) with a compass.

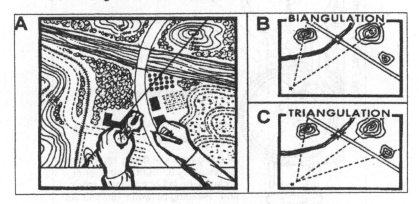

**Triangulation**

(a) Try to use 3 or more azimuths.

(b) Positively identify a major land feature and determine a line of position (LOP).

(c) Check map orientation each time compass is used.

(d) Plot the LOP using a thin stick or blade of grass (combat) or pencil line (non-combat).

(e) Repeat steps (**b**) through (**d**) for other LOPs.

e. Use the compass for night navigation by—

(1) Setting up compass for night navigation.

(2) Aligning north-seeking arrow with luminous line and follow front of compass.

(3) Using point-to-point navigation.

f. Route selection techniques follow:

(1) Circumnavigation.

(a) Find a prominent landmark on the opposite side of the obstacle.

(b) Contour around obstacle to landmark.

(c) Resume your route of travel.

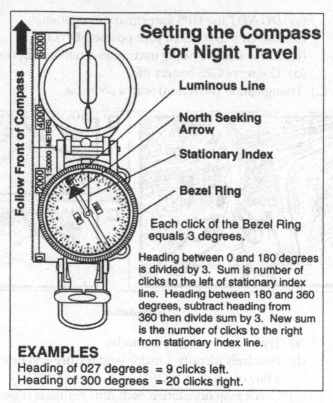

**Setting the Compass for Night Travel**

Luminous Line

North Seeking Arrow

Stationary Index

Bezel Ring

Each click of the Bezel Ring equals 3 degrees.

Heading between 0 and 180 degrees is divided by 3. Sum is number of clicks to the left of stationary index line. Heading between 180 and 360 degrees, subtract heading from 360 then divide sum by 3. New sum is the number of clicks to the right from stationary index line.

**EXAMPLES**
Heading of 027 degrees = 9 clicks left.
Heading of 300 degrees = 20 clicks right.

Compass Night Navigation Setup

(2) Dogleg and 90 degree offset.
(3) Straight-line heading as follows:
    (a) Maintain heading until reaching destination.
    (b) Measure distance by counting the number of paces in a given course and convert to map units.
       • One pace is the distance covered each time the same foot touches the ground.
       • Distances measured by paces are approximate (example in open terrain, 900 paces per kilometer [average], or example in rough terrain, 1200 paces per kilometer [average]).
    (c) Use pace count in conjunction with terrain evaluation and heading to determine location. An individual's pace varies because of factors such as steep terrain,

day/night travel, or injured/uninjured condition. Adjust estimation of distance traveled against these factors to get relative accuracy when using a pace count

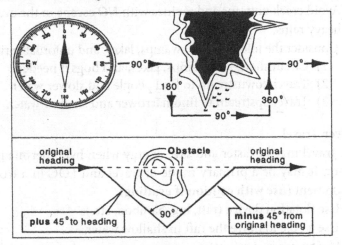

**Dogleg and 90 Degree Offset**

   (4)  Deliberate offset is—
      (a)  Used when finding a point on a linear feature (that is road or river).
      (b)  Intentionally navigated to left or right of target so you know which way to turn at the linear feature.
   (5)  Point-to-point is same as straight line.
      (a)  Pick out landmarks on the heading and walk the trail of least resistance to a point.
      (b)  On reaching a point, establish another landmark and continue.

## 3. Travel Considerations
  a.  Pick the easiest and safest route (non-combat).
  b.  Maintain a realistic pace; take rest stops when needed.
  c.  Avoid overdressing and overheating.
  d.  Consider food and water requirements.
  e.  Take special care of feet (change socks regularly).
  f.  Pack equipment to prevent loss, damage, pack imbalance, and personal safety.

g. Go **around** obstacles, not over or through them.

h. Travel on trails whenever possible (non-combat).

i. Travel in forested areas if possible.

j. Avoid creek bottoms and ravines with *NO* escape in the event of heavy rains.

k. Consider the following for swamps, lakes, and unfordable rivers:
   (1) Circumnavigate swamps, lakes, and bogs if needed.
   (2) Travel downstream to find people and slower water.
   (3) Travel upstream to find narrower and shallow water.

## 4. River Travel

River travel may be faster and save energy when hypothermia is not a factor. It may be a primary mode of travel and LOC in a tropical environment (**use with caution if evading**).

a. Use flotation device (raft, log, bamboo, etc.).

b. Use a pole to move the raft in shallow water.

c. Use an oar in deep water.

d. Stay near inside edge of river bends (current speed is less).

e. Keep near shore.

f. Watch for the following *DANGERS*:
   (1) Snags.
   (2) Sweepers (overhanging limbs and trees).
   (3) Rapids (*DO NOT* attempt to shoot the rapids).
   (4) Waterfalls.
   (5) Hazardous animals.

g. Consider using a flotation device when crossing rivers or large/deep streams.

## 5. Ice and Snow Travel

Travel should be limited to areas free of hazards.

a. *DO NOT* travel in—
   (1) Blizzards.
   (2) Bitterly cold winds.
   (3) Poor visibility.

b. Obstacles to winter travel follow:
   (1) Reduced daylight hours (*BE AWARE*).

(2) Deep soft snow (if movement is necessary, make snowshoes). Travel is easier in early morning or late afternoon near dusk when snow is frozen or crusted.

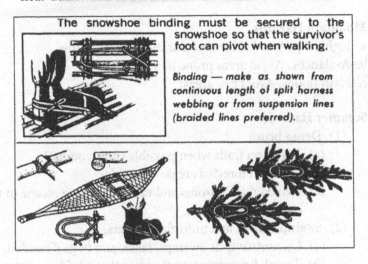

The snowshoe binding must be secured to the snowshoe so that the survivor's foot can pivot when walking.

*Binding — make as shown from continuous length of split harness webbing or from suspension lines (braided lines preferred).*

**Improvised Snowshoes**

(3) Avalanche prone areas to avoid:
   (a) Slopes 30–45 degrees or greater.
   (b) Trees without uphill branches (identifies prior avalanches).
   (c) Heavy snow loading on ridge tops.
(4) If caught in an avalanche, do the following:
   (a) Backstroke to decrease burial depth.
   (b) Move hand around tace to create air pocket as moving snow slows.
(5) Frozen water crossings.
   (a) Weak ice should be expected where—
      • Rivers are straight.
      • Objects protrude through ice.
      • Snow banks extend over the ice.
      • Rivers or streams come together.
      • Water vapor rising indicates open or warm areas.
   (b) Air pockets form when a frozen river loses volume.

(c) When crossing frozen water, distribute your weight by laying flat, belly crawling, or using snowshoes.
c.  Glacier travel is hazardous and should be avoided.

## 6. Mountain Hazards
a.  Lightning. Avoid ridge tops during thunderstorms.
b.  Avalanche. Avoid areas prone to avalanches.
c.  Flash floods. Avoid low areas.

## 7. Summer Hazards
(1)  Dense brush.
   (a)  Travel on trails when possible (non-combat).
   (b)  Travel in forested areas if possible.
   (c)  Avoid creek bottoms and ravines with no escape in the event of heavy rains.
(2)  Swamps, lakes, and unfordable rivers.
   (a)  Circumnavigate swamps, lakes, and bogs if needed.
   (b)  Travel downstream to find people and slower water.
   (c)  Travel upstream to find narrower and shallow water.

## 8. Dry Climates
a.  *DO NOT* travel unless certain of reaching the destination using the water supply available.
b.  Travel at dawn or dusk on hot days.
c.  Follow the easiest trail possible (non-combat), avoiding—
   (1)  Deep sandy dune areas.
   (2)  Rough terrain.
d  In sand dune areas—
   (1)  Follow hard valley floor between dunes.
   (2)  Travel on the windward side of dune ridges.
e.  If a sandstorm occurs—
   (1)  Mark your direction of travel.
   (2)  Sit or lie down in direction of travel.
   (3)  Try to get to the downwind side of natural shelter.
   (4)  Cover the mouth and nose with a piece of cloth.

(5) Protect the eyes.

(6) Remain stationary until the storm is over.

## 9.Tropical climates

a. Travel only when it is light.

b. Avoid obstacles like thickets and swamps.

c. Part the vegetation to pass through. Avoid grabbing vegetation; it may have spines or thorns (**use gloves** if possible).

d. *DO NOT* climb over logs if you can go around them.

e. Find trails—

(1) Where 2 streams meet.

(2) Where a low pass goes over a range of hills.

f. While traveling trails—

(1) Watch for disturbed areas on game trails; they may indicate a pitfall or trap.

(2) Use a walking stick to probe for pitfalls or traps.

(3) *DO NOT* sleep on the trail.

(4) Exercise caution, the enemy uses the trails also.

## 10. Open Seas

a. Using currents—

(1) Deploy sea anchor. Sea anchor may be adjusted to make use of existing currents.

(2) Sit low in the raft.

(3) Deflate the raft slightly so it rides lower in the water.

b. Using winds—

(1) Pull in sea anchor.

(2) Inflate raft so it rides higher.

(3) Sit up in raft so body catches the wind.

(4) Construct a shade cover/sail. (Sail aids in making landfall.)

c. Making landfall. Indications of land are—

(1) Fixed cumulus clouds in a clear sky or in a cloudy sky where all other clouds are moving.

(2) Greenish tint in the sky (**in the tropics**).

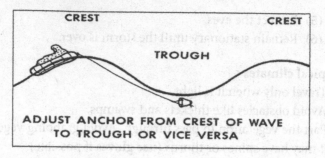

Anchor Deployment

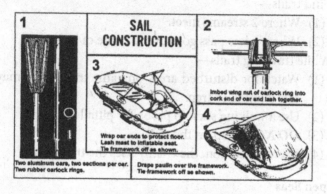

Shade/Sail Construction

(3) Lighter colored reflection on clouds (open water causes dark gray reflections) (**in the arctic**).
(4) Lighter colored water (indicates shallow water).
(5) The odors and sounds.
   (a) Odors from swamps and smoke.
   (b) Roar of surf/bird cries coming from one direction.
(6) Directional flights of birds at dawn and at dusk.
 d. Swimming ashore—
(1) Consider physical condition.
(2) Use a flotation aid.
(3) Secure all gear to body before reaching landfall.
(4) Remain in raft as long as possible.
(5) Use the sidestroke or breaststroke to conserve strength if thrown from raft.

(6) Wear footgear and at least 1 layer of clothing.

(7) Try to make landfall during the lull between the sets of waves (waves are generally in **sets** of 7, from **smallest** to **largest**).

(8) In moderate surf.

    (a) Swim forward on the back of a wave.

    (b) Make a shallow dive just before the wave breaks to end the ride.

(9) In high surf.

    (a) Swim shoreward in the trough between waves.

    (b) When the seaward wave approaches, face it and submerge.

    (c) After it passes, work shoreward in the next trough.

(10) If caught in the undertow of a large wave—

    (a) Remain calm and swim to the surface.

    (b) Lie as close to the surface as possible.

    (c) Parallel shoreline and attempt landfall at a point further down shore.

(11) Select a landing point.

    (a) Avoid places where waves explode upon rocks.

    (b) Find a place where waves smoothly rush onto the rocks.

(12) After selecting a landing site—

    (a) Face shoreward.

    (b) Assume a sitting position with feet 2 or 3 feet lower than head to absorb the shock of hitting submerged objects.

e. Rafting ashore—

    (1) Select landing point carefully.

    (2) Use caution landing when the sun is low and straight in front of you causing poor visibility.

    (3) Land on the lee (downwind) side of islands or point of land if possible.

    (4) Head for gaps in the surf line.

    (5) Penetrate surfby—

        (a) Taking down most shade/sails.

        (b) Using paddles to maintain control.

        (c) Deploying a sea anchor for stability.

**CAUTION:** *DO NOT* deploy a sea anchor if traveling through coral.

   f. Making sea ice landings on large stable ice flows. Icebergs, small flows, and disintegrating flows are dangerous (ice can cut a raft).
- (1) Use paddles to avoid sharp edges.
- (2) Store raft away from the ice edge.
- (3) Keep raft inflated and ready for use.
- (4) Weight down/secure raft so it does not blow away.

## CHAPTER 5

# CLOUDS: FORETELLERS OF WEATHER

About 200 years ago an Englishman classified clouds according to what they looked like to a person seeing them from the ground. He grouped them into three classes and gave them Latin names: cirrus, cumulus, and stratus. These three names, alone and combined with other Latin words, are still used to identify different cloud formations.

By being familiar with the different cloud formations and what weather they portend, you can take appropriate action for your protection.

Courtesy of National Oceanic and Atmospheric Administration

## CIRRUS CLOUDS

Cirrus clouds are the very high clouds that look like thin streaks or curls. They are usually 6 kilometers or more above the earth and are usually a sign of fair weather. In cold climates, however, cirrus clouds that begin to multiply and are accompanied by increasing winds blowing steadily from a northerly direction indicate an oncoming blizzard.

Courtesy of National Oceanic and Atmospheric Administration

# CUMULUS CLOUDS

Cumulus clouds are fluffy, white, heaped-up clouds. These clouds, which are much lower than cirrus clouds, are often fair weather clouds. They are apt to appear around midday on a sunny day, looking like large cotton balls with flat bottoms. As the day advances, they may become bigger and push higher into the atmosphere, piling up to appear like a mountain of clouds. These can turn into storm clouds.

Courtesy of National Oceanic and Atmospheric Administration

# STRATUS CLOUDS

Stratus clouds are very low, gray clouds, often making an even gray layer over the whole sky. These clouds generally mean rain.

Courtesy of National Oceanic and Atmospheric Administration

# NIMBUS CLOUDS

Nimbus clouds are rain clouds of uniform grayness that extend over the entire sky.

Courtesy of National Oceanic and Atmospheric Administration

# CUMULONIMBUS CLOUDS

Cumulonimbus is the cloud formation resulting from a cumulus cloud building up, extending to great heights, and forming in the shape of an anvil. You can expect a thunderstorm if this cloud is moving in your direction.

Courtesy of National Oceanic and Atmospheric Administration

# CIRROSTRATUS CLOUDS

Cirrostratus is a fairly uniform layer of high stratus clouds that are darker than cirrus clouds. Cirrostratus clouds indicate good weather.

Courtesy of National Oceanic and Atmospheric Administration

# CIRROCUMULUS CLOUDS

Cirrocumulus is a small, white, round cloud at a high altitude. Cirrocumulus clouds indicate good weather.

# SCUDS

A loose, vapory cloud (scud) driven before the wind is a sign of continuing bad weather.

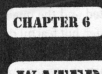

# CHAPTER 6

# WATER

"Water is the driving force of all nature."

*—Leonardo Da Vinci*

Getting lost or stranded in the wild is something that can happen to anyone, whether you're a Navy SEAL, experienced outdoorsmen, hiker, tourist, or just someone out for a weekend drive. Anybody can be forced to deal with circumstances beyond their control, alone and lost, with only their wits to rely on for survival.

The human body is composed of up to seventy-eight percent water. So it's no surprise that the single-most important thing you need to live is not food; it's water. The good news is that if you're resourceful and know where to look, you can find or collect good drinking water in just about any environment on earth.

The Institute of Medicine currently recommends a daily intake of approximately 2 to 2 ½ quarts of water to replace the water lost through normal body functions—urination, defecation, breathing, and sweating. All of the chemical and electrical activities that take place in the human body take place in a water environment; when water is in short supply, these activities begin to malfunction.

It's important to understand that many people begin their survival already dehydrated due to stress and other factors. They often continue to dehydrate further when water supplies are limited and the quality of any available water is suspect. People needing water, but fearful that it is contaminated with *Giardia, Cryptosporidium,* or other harmful pathogens, often put off drinking or choose not to use the water at all.

## IN NORTH AMERICA, AS A GENERAL RULE, IT IS BETTER TO DRINK AVAILABLE FRESH WATER.

If the water contains harmful pathogens, the onset of symptoms will usually be days, if not weeks away. By then the individual will hopefully have access to medical care.

The one exception to this rule is that certain lakes mainly found in the western United States contain high concentrations of calcium carbonate and calcium bicarbonate. This water is not potable. Lakes containing these substances are usually easy to identify because the calcium salts leached from the soil are deposited in the form of white powder around the shorelines. This water tastes terrible and should not be consumed unless there is absolutely no other water source available.

**IN OTHER PARTS OF THE WORLD, ESPECIALLY DEVELOP-
ING COUNTRIES, DRINKING WATER THAT HAS NOT BEEN
DISINFECTED IS NOT RECOMMENDED.**
Viruses such as hepatitis, not commonly found in North American
waters, are prevalent here and can quickly cause incapacitating illness.

## FINDING WATER

Throughout much of North America, fresh water can usually be
found in open sources such as lakes, ponds, rivers, and streams. In
most cases, it can be obtained fairly easily. Remember that water always seeks the lowest level possible and that, if present, some form of
vegetation will most likely grow nearby.

The best way to locate water is from a vantage point that allows you
to scan the surrounding countryside. Slowly and methodically look
for indicators such as green vegetation, flocks of birds, trails left by
domestic and wild animals, and even large formations of rock that
can contain natural springs. Check for low-lying areas—such as depressions or sinks—where rainfall or melting snow is likely to collect.
Water can often be found in these areas long after the last precipitation, especially if they are shaded.

Water sources like these should be checked carefully since they're
often contaminated with debris that has been washed into the
drainage. Finding the remains of animals that have died nearby or

in the water and other similar contaminants will necessitate boiling the water, the use of halogens (iodine or chlorine), or the use of a mechanical purification pump.

The quantity of water produced by seeps and springs tends to vary greatly. Some of them produce no more than a few teaspoons of water per hour. In other cases, gallons of water can flow from the ground in minutes. Where the output is slow and small, use the flat edge of the mouth on a plastic bag to scoop up the water from a shallow source; if it is flowing, use it to collect the water as it runs into the bag. A short piece of vinyl aquarium hose also works well for sucking up water from shallow collections or to recover water from narrow cracks in the rocks.

Also, keep an eye out for man-made sources of water such as windmills, wells, tanks, dams, and irrigation canals. Windmills are common in parts of North America, especially in areas where little surface water exists. In most cases, the water pumped to the surface is collected in a nearby tank or pumped directly into a trough from which livestock can drink. Where an open source is not available, it may be necessary to dismantle the piping associated with the windmill to gain access to the water.

If you find an abandoned well where the rope and bucket typically used to lift water from these wells is missing, improvise a means to lower a container down into the well to retrieve the water. If you don't have a container, an item of clothing can be lowered into the water to serve as a sponge.

In arid areas, particularly in the western and southwestern United States, many state wildlife agencies and conservation organizations have installed rainwater collectors called "guzzlers." These are designed to gather precipitation and feed it into a holding tank, where it remains until it is either consumed by animals or evaporates.

Just because there's no water visible on the surface of the ground, that doesn't mean that it's not present in the soil in sufficient quantity to be collected. Locate low-lying areas where water is most likely to have accumulated and dig down until damp layers of soil are found. The hole should be about a foot in diameter. Over time, water may seep into the hole where it can be collected. If no indicators of sub-surface water are present, dig a hole in the outside bend of a dry riverbed. Look for a location where the centrifugal force of flowing water has eroded the outer bend, creating a depression where the last remnants of water flowing downriver will have accumulated.

Groundwater collected this way is likely to be muddy, but straining it through cloth will clean it and will get you by in the short term. It's important to remember that you're taking a risk anytime you drink ground water without purifying it.

Rain is a great source of drinking water and in most rural areas can be consumed without risk of disease or illness. If you have a poncho or some plastic sheeting, spread it out and tie the corners to trees a few feet off the ground. Find a container and tie the plastic on a slant so that the rainwater can drain into it. If you can't find a container, de-vise a makeshift water bag by tying the plastic level on all four corners but letting it sag in the middle so that the rainwater can collect there. If the rainwater tastes different than what you're used to, it's because it lacks the minerals that are found in groundwater and in streams. If you don't have a poncho, rain gear, or piece of plastic, remember that water will collect on the upper surfaces of any material (it doesn't have to be waterproof) and drain to the lowest point, where it can be collected in a bucket or other container.

Melt snow before you consume it because if you eat it frozen, you'll reduce your body temperature, which can lead to dehydration. The best technique to convert snow into water is by using what military survival schools call a water machine. Make a bag out of any available porous fabric (you can use a T-shirt), fill it with snow, and hang it near (but not directly over) a fire. Place a container under the bag to collect the water. By continually filling the bag with snow you'll keep it from burning.

If your circumstances don't allow you to make a fire, you can melt snow with the heat of your body. But the process is slow. Put several cups of snow in any available waterproof container (preferably a soft plastic water bag, locking sandwich bag, or something similar) and place it between layers of your clothing or in your sleeping bag. Since the amount of heat needed to convert snow to water is large and the amount of body heat available is finite, only small quantities can be melted at a time.

# COLLECTING WATER

Heavy dew can be a good source of potable water. Before the sun rises, tie absorbent cloth around your shins and walk through high grass. This way you might be able to collect enough water for an early morning drink.

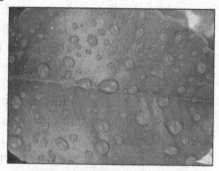

Water droplets collecting on leaf.

## BAMBOO

Fruits, coconuts, cacti, vines, palm trees, and bamboo can also be good sources of liquid sustenance. Bend the top of a green bamboo stalk down about a foot off the ground and tie it off. Cut a few inches off the tip, put a container underneath, and leave it overnight. The next day, you're likely to find a nice amount of clear, drinkable water.

Drinking water out of bamboo.

## VINES

Water-producing vines varying in size from the diameter of a pencil up to the thickness of a man's forearm can be found throughout much of the southeastern United States. The thicker the vine, the more water it is capable of producing. Select the thickest one first.

Use a sharp knife or a machete to sever the tough, woody vine. Vines that exude a white latex sap or those that produce a colored or foul-smelling sap should be avoided. If no sap is observed, or if the sap that is observed is clear and without aroma, remove a twenty-four-inch section, severing the

Bamboo is a good source of liquid sustenance.

higher end first and then the lower end. If the lower end is cut first, the water contained within the vine is drawn up by capillary action and far less water will drain out by the time the upper end is severed.

Once removed, hold the section of vine vertically and the water in it will drain into a container (or a cupped hand), where it should be evaluated. Any liquid that is colored should not be consumed. Liquid that has an unpleasant aroma other than a faint "woody" smell should not be consumed but can be used to

Drinking water out of a vine.

satisfy any hygiene needs. Taste a small amount of the water. Water that has a disagreeable flavor other than a slightly "earthy" or "woody" taste should not be utilized for drinking. Hold a small amount of water in your mouth for a few moments to determine if there is any burning or other disagreeable sensation. If any irritation occurs, the water should be discarded. Liquid that looks like water, smells like water, and tastes like water is water and can be safely consumed in large quantities without further purification.

## CACTUS
Cactus as a source of water is often overrated. But if you decide to approach one, use caution, as the thorns usually cause infections.

Use sharp sticks or knifes to handle cactus safely. Any injury from a cactus plant should be treated immediately to reduce the risk of infection.

Although all cacti can be used for gaining additional moisture, it can take a great deal of work to open a full-sized barrow cactus and fight with the spiny thorns that protect it. If you decide to take on a cactus, do it in the cool of the evening. Using caution, remove the top of the barrow cactus. Once the top is off, you will find a white substance that resembles watermelon meat inside (this is a liquid-filled inner tissue). Using your knife, cut out hand-size chunks and squeeze the moisture from them.

The thicker the vine, the more water it is capable of producing.

Prickly pears are easier to collect and prepare. Use a large sharp stick and a good knife. Stab the round prickly pear with the stick, and then cut it off with the knife. Next, use a fire to burn the thorns off of the cactus. Make sure you sear the cactus well to remove even the smallest thorns.

Although overrated, cacti can still be used as a water source in a pinch.

Once the thorns are removed, peel the green- or purple-colored outer substance off, and eat the inside. Prickly pear meat tastes so good that in Arizona and New Mexico people make jellies and candies from it. Chew the moisture-filled inner tissue, not the rough outer "bark."

# GETTING WATER FROM PLANTS

The use of clear plastic bags to enclose living vegetation and capture the moisture transpired by the leaves can be an effective method of collecting water. A plant's survival is dependent on its ability to gather water from the soil. This water is passed up through the plant's roots, stems, and branches, and is finally released back to the atmosphere through pores in the leaves as water vapor—a process called evapotranspiration.

This water vapor can be collected with a clear plastic bag. It works best when the vegetation is high enough to be off the ground. Shake the vegetation to remove any insects, bird droppings, or other materials that might contaminate the water. Insert the limb or bush just like you would a hand into a mitten. Then, tie the open end of the bag around the tree or bush and seal the opening shut with a cord or duct tape. At the closed end of the bag, tie a rock so the bag is weighted and forms a collection point for the water.

Within a short period of time, water will begin to condense on the inner surface of the bag, collect into water droplets, and drain to the lowest point of the bag. The quantity of water obtained in this manner is dependent on the amount of water in the ground and the type of vegetation used. Other factors that will determine water production include the amount of sunlight available (it doesn't work at night), the clarity of the plastic bag, and the length of time the process is allowed to work. It is not uncommon to find that two or three cups of water, and sometimes much more, have accumulated over a six- to eight-hour daylight period.

The best way to remove the water without disturbing the bag is to insert a length of vinyl aquarium hose through the neck of the bag down to the lowest point where water will collect. The water can then be sucked out or siphoned into a container. When enclosing vegetation in the plastic bag, it is advisable to place a small stone in the lower corner where the water will collect. The weight of the stone creates a separation between the enclosed plant life and the water and will keep plant saps from contaminating the water.

Similarly, leaves and small branches can be cut and placed in a clear plastic bag. In this method, heat from the sun causes the liquids in the foliage to be extracted and collect in the bag. However, this method may produce water containing unsafe toxins. Taste it first. If the water is bitter, do not drink it.

# SOLAR STILLS

The quantity of water produced by a solar still depends on the amount of water contained in the ground. Because of this, solar stills are not reliable for obtaining water in arid areas since desert soils tend to hold little or no water. The amount that a survivor is likely to obtain via this method must

Solar stills are not reliable methods for collecting water in arid areas.

be balanced against the amount of sweat lost while constructing the device. However, in other types of climates, a solar still can be very effective way of capturing water.

To build a solar still, dig a hole approximately one meter across and two feet deep. Dig a smaller hole, or slump, in the middle of the hole. Place a container in the slump to collect the water. Then, cover the hole with a plastic sheet and secure the edges of the sheet with sand and rocks. Finally, place a rock in the center of the sheet, so it sags.

During daylight hours the temperature in the hole will rise due to the heat of the sun, thereby creating heat vapors which will condensate on the inside of the plastic sheet and run down. It then drops into the container in the sump hole.

## YOU SHOULD NEVER DRINK THE FOLLOWING:

- Blood
- Urine
- Saltwater
- Alcohol
- Fresh sea ice

Fresh sea ice is milky or grey, has sharp edges, does not break easily, and is extremely salty. Older sea ice is usually salt-free, has a blue or black tint and rounded edges, and breaks easily. Melted old sea ice is usually safe to drink, but should be purified first, if possible.

# WATERBORNE CONTAMINANTS

In most parts of the world, surface water is seldom pure. There are five basic waterborne contaminants that you should be particularly aware of: turbidity, toxic chemicals, bacteria, viruses, and parasitic worms.

## TURBIDITY

A measure of the cloudiness of water, or more specifically a measure of the extent to which the intensity of light passing through water is reduced by suspended matter in the water. The sources of turbidity can be attributable to suspended and colloidal material, and may be caused by several factors such as: microorganisms and organic detritus, silica and other sands and substances including zinc, iron and manganese compounds, clay or silt, the result of natural processes of erosion and/or as waste from various industries.

## TOXIC CHEMICALS

Dangerous and toxic chemicals include, among others, pesticides, herbicides, fertilizers from agricultural land and runoff from household and industrial chemicals.

## BACTERIA, VIRUSES, PARASITIC WORMS

*Giardia lamblia* is a parasite that lives in the intestines of humans and animals. It's expelled from the body in feces, and is found worldwide and in every region of the United States. It causes giardiasis, which produces cramping, nausea, and diarrhea. Symptoms may not show up for two weeks, and once present can last as long as six weeks. If infected, get medical attention as soon as possible.

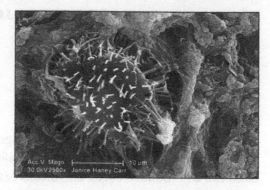

Giardia parasites can be found in lakes, ponds, rivers and streams worldwide.

*Cryptosporidiosis* is another waterborne illness caused by parasites found in feces. The same symptoms as giardiasis can be expected, but more severe. Both of these parasites can be found in soil and vegetation as well, so wash anything you plan on eating in purified water and remember: To give yourself the best chance at survival, always boil your water, even if it looks clean.

# WATER PURIFICATION AND DISINFECTION

To be safe to drink, water must be disinfected so that all harmful microorganisms are removed. To do this water must be boiled, treated with chemicals, or filtered. "Disinfection" of water should not be confused with "purification" of water. Some of the methods used to purify water may not remove or kill enough of the pathogens to ensure your safety. Make sure the water you drink is disinfected.

The first step to disinfecting water is to select the cleanest, clearest source of water available. Inorganic and organic materials such as clay, silt, plankton, plant debris, and other microscopic organisms will reduce the effectiveness of either chemical or filtration disinfection. Chemicals used to disinfect water will clump to any particulate in the water, thus reducing its ability to disinfect the water. And water containing a lot of material will quickly clog a filtration system. For the best results, collect water from below the surface but not off the bottom. When collecting murky water, allow it to settle and then filter it through your shirttail, bandanna, or other piece of cloth.

## REMEMBER:

**Filtering** water doesn't always purify it, but it does reduce particles and sediment and make the water taste better. However, there are microbial purification filters on the market that not only remove parasites such as Giardia, but also kill waterborne bacteria and viruses. These types of filters are optimal.

- **Boiling** is the best way of killing all microorganisms. Boiling will not neutralize chemical pollutants.
- To purify water with **chemicals**, use water purification tablets.

## BOILING

Bringing water to a boil kills any organisms in it. In most cases, water does not have to be boiled for a specific length of time. The time it takes to bring water to a boil and the temperature of the water when it boils is sufficient to kill *Giardia*, *Cryptosporidium*, and any other waterborne pathogens. While the boiling point of water decreases as you climb higher, the temperature at which the water boils is still hot enough to kill those organisms that might make you sick. Continuing to boil the water wastes fuel, evaporates the water, and delays consumption.

Boil water to destroy any waterborne pathogens.

Overseas, especially in developing countries where river systems are still a frequent method of sewage disposal, boiling for a longer period of time (one or two minutes) is advisable.

# CHEMICAL PURIFICATION

Chemicals that have the ability to disinfect water are known as halogens, and include iodine and chlorine. The effectiveness of halogens is directly related to their concentration, the amount of time they are left in contact with the water, and the temperature of the water—the colder the water the longer the contact time.

## IODINE

Comes in tablet and liquid forms. I recommend the tablets because liquid iodine is messy and the containers are prone to leaking. Potable Aqua tablets (which contain iodine) are used by the U.S. military and many disaster relief agencies.

Iodine kills harmful bacteria, viruses, and most protozoan cysts found in untreated water. (It is NOT effective on *Cryptosporidium*.) The recommend dosage of two tablets per quart or liter of water is sufficient to kill organisms such as *Giardia*. Once the tablets are placed in the water, they should be allowed to sit for at least thirty minutes (even longer if the water is very cold), and then shaken so that the iodine and water mix thoroughly. The dissolved tablets will leave a slight iodine taste in the water, which some find disagreeable. Lemon juice, lemonade, Kool-Aid, or Gatorade powder can be added to neutralize the iodine flavor.

Iodine tablets are commonly packaged with a second bottle of ascorbic acid (PA Plus) tablets that deactivate the iodine, making the water pleasant to drink. One tablet is usually enough to reduce the iodine taste.

Iodine tablets deteriorate on exposure to heat, humidity, or moisture. Over time, opening and closing the cap to remove tablets results in the normally gray-colored tablets changing to green or yellow. Once they have changed color, they have lost their effectiveness and shouldn't be used. Avoid using the military iodine tablets that are sometimes found in military surplus stores. The military got rid of them because their shelf life has expired.

**Advantage of iodine tablets:**
- Easy to use
- Lightweight
- Inexpensive

**Disadvantages:**
- Not effective against *Cryptosporidium* cysts
- Some people are allergic to iodine
- People with known thyroid problems should not use iodine
- Iodine should not be used as a long-term (more than six weeks) method of purifying water due to its potential harmful effects on the thyroid.

# CHLORINE

An effective agent against bacteria, viruses, and, unlike iodine, cysts such as *Cryptosporidium*. Another advantage of using chlorine is that it leaves no aftertaste. On the downside, a significant disadvantage of using chlorine tablets is that you have to wait for four hours after adding a tablet before you can drink the water.

**Advantages of Chlorine tablets:**
- No aftertaste
- Chlorine kills *Cryptosporidium*

**Disadvantages:**
- Four-hour contact time

Almost all laundry bleaches, including Clorox, contain five and one-half percent sodium hypoclorite, which is a suitable purification chemical for water. Put a small amount in a bottle with an eyedropper dispenser and add it to your E&E kit. Make sure you do not use powdered, scented, or other non-pure bleaches.

Before adding bleach to the water you want to purify, remove all suspended material by filtration (through a cotton cloth, improvised sand filter, or other means) or by simply allowing sediment to settle to the bottom.

Add eight drops of bleach per gallon of water (or two drops per quart). If the water was filtered, then shake it up to evenly dispense the bleach, and wait fifteen minutes. If the water has sediment on the bottom, don't shake it up. Instead, allow the treated water to stand for thirty minutes.

Because killing microorganisms also consumes the bleach, you can tell by smelling whether or not there's anything left to kill. If there's no chlorine odor then all of the bleach was used up, meaning there could still be living organisms. Repeat the dosage and allow the water to stand for another fifteen minutes. If there is any chlorine odor, however faint, after thirty minutes, all of the bacteria, viruses, and other microorganisms are dead, and the bleach has done its job with some to spare.

When treating cloudy, green, or really nasty water (swamp water, for example), start with sixteen drops of bleach per gallon of water (or four drops per quart). Smell the water. If there's a faint odor of chlorine, the water is drinkable. If not, then repeat the treatment.

The Lifestraw eliminates 100 percent of waterborne bacteria, ninty-nine percent of viruses, and particles as small as fifteen microns.

## TREATING LARGER QUANTITIES OF WATER

A teaspoon of bleach treats about 7 ½ gallons of clear water or about four gallons of dirty water. Therefore, a tablespoon of bleach treats about twenty gallons of clear water or about ten gallons of dirty water. A quarter cup of bleach will purify about ninety gallons of clear water or forty-five gallons of dirty water.

## LIFESTRAW

The LifeStraw is a portable filtration device that enables you to safely drink directly from any fresh water source. The straw itself is about eleven inches long, less than one inch around, and looks like a jumbo drinking straw. One end has the narrow mouthpiece; the other goes directly into the water source. Each LifeStraw lasts for 185 gallons, roughly the amount of water needed for one person per year.

The filter is designed to eliminate 100 percent of waterborne bacteria, almost ninety-nine percent of viruses, and particles as small as fifteen microns.

## CHAPTER 7

# FOOD

## 1. FOOD PROCUREMENT

### A. SOURCES AND LOCATION.

(1) Mammals can be found where—
   (a) Trails lead to watering, feeding, and bedding areas.
   (b) Droppings or tracks look fresh.

(2) Birds can be found by—
   (a) Observing the direction of flight in the early morning and late afternoon (leads to feeding, watering, and roosting areas).
   (b) Listening for bird noises (indication of nesting areas).

(3) Fish and other marine life locations.

(4) Reptiles and amphibians are found almost worldwide.

1 OVERHANGING BRUSH
2 UNDERCUT
3 POOL FROM BACKWASH
4 FEEDER STREAM
5 BEHIND ROCKS
6 FALLEN TREE

**Fishing Locations**

   (5)  Insects are found—
- (a)  In dead logs and stumps.
- (b)  At ant and termite mounds.
- (c)  On ponds, lakes, and slow moving streams.

## B. PROCUREMENT TECHNIQUES.
   (1)  Snares-
- (a)  Work while unattended.
- (b)  Location:
  - Trails leading to water, feeding, and bedding areas.
  - Mouth of dens.

**Snare Placement**

- (c)  Construction of simple loop snare.
  - Use materials that will not break under the strain of holding an animal.
  - Use a figure 8 (locking loop) if wire is used.
    - • once tightened, the wire locks in place, preventing reopening, and the animal's escape.
  - To construct a squirrel pole use simple loop snares.
  - Make noose opening slightly larger than the animal's head (**3-finger** width for squirrels, **fist-sized** for rabbits).
- (d)  Placement of snares (set as many as possible).
  - Avoid disturbing the area.
  - Use funneling (natural or improvised).

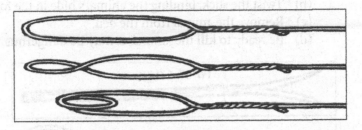

**Locking Loop**

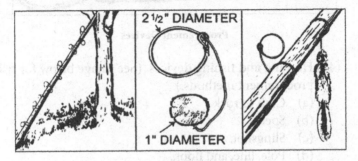

2 1/2" DIAMETER

1" DIAMETER

**Squirrel Poel**

FUNNELING

**Funneling**

  (2)  Noose stick (easier and safer to use than the hands).

  (3)  Twist stick.

      (a)  Insert forked stick into a den until something soft is met.

(b) Twist the stick, binding the animal's hide in the fork.

(c) Remove the animal from the den.

(d) Be ready to **kill** the animal; **it may be dangerous**.

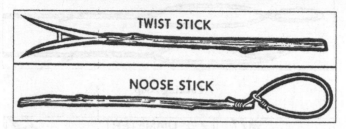

**Procurement Devices**

(4) Hunting and fishing devices. (See image below for fishing procurement methods.)

(a) Club or rock.

(b) Spear.

(c) Slingshot.

(d) Pole, line, and hook.

(e) Net.

(f) Trap.

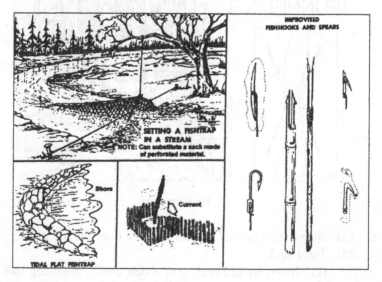

**Procurement Methods**

(5) Precautions:
   (a) Wear shoes to protect the feet when wading in water.
   (b) Avoid reaching into dark holes.
   (c) **Kill** animals before handling. Animals in distress may attract the enemy.
   (d) *DO NOT* secure fishing lines to yourself or the raft.
   (e) **Kill** fish before bringing them into the raft.
   (f) *DO NOT* eat fish with—
      • Spines.
      • Unpleasant odor.
      • Pale, slimy gills.
      • Sunken eyes.
      • Flabby skin.
      • Flesh that remains dented when pressed.
   (g) *DO NOT* eat fish eggs or liver (entrails).
   (h) Avoid all crustaceans above the high tide mark.
   (i) Avoid cone-shaped shells.

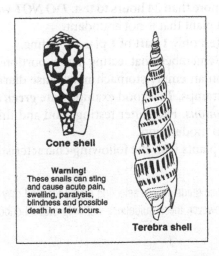

**Cone -Shaped Shells of Venomous Snails**

   (j) Avoid hairy insects; the hairs could cause irritation or infection.
   (k) Avoid poisonous insects, for example:
      • Centipedes.

- Scorpions.
- Poisonous spiders.

(l) Avoid disease carrying insects, such as—
- Flies.
- Mosquitoes.
- Ticks.

**C. PLANT FOODS.** *Before using the following guide use your evasion chart to identify edible plants:*

> **Note:** If you cannot positively identify an edible plant and choose to try an unknown plant, these guidelines may help determine edibility.

(1) Selection criteria.
  (a) Before testing for edibility, ensure there are enough plants to make testing worth your time and effort. Each part of a plant (roots, leaves, stems, bark, etc.) requires more than 24 hours to test. *DO NOT* waste time testing a plant that is not abundant.
  (b) Test only 1 part of 1 plant at a time.
  (c) Remember that eating large portions of plant food on an empty stomach may cause diarrhea, nausea, or cramps. *Two* good examples are *green apples* and *wild onions*. Even after testing food and finding it safe, eat in moderation.

(2) Avoid plants with the following characteristics:

> **Note:** Using these guidelines in selecting plants for food may eliminate some edible plants; however, these guidelines will help prevent choosing potentially toxic plants.

  (a) Milky sap (dandelion has milky sap but is safe to eat and easily recognizable).
  (b) Spines, fine hairs, and thorns (skin irritants/contact dermatitis). *Prickly pear* and *thistles* are exceptions. *Bracken fern fiddleheads* also violate this guideline.

(c) Mushrooms and fungus.
(d) Umbrella shaped flowers (hemlock is eliminated).
(e) Bulbs (*only* onions smell like onions).
(f) Grain heads with pink, purplish, or black spurs.
(g) Beans, bulbs, or seeds inside pods.
(h) Old or wilted leaves.
(i) Plants with shiny leaves.
(j) White and yellow berries. (Aggregate berries such as black and dewberries are always edible, test all others before eating.)
(k) Almond scent in woody parts and leaves.

## D. TEST PROCEDURES.

**CAUTION:** Test all parts of the plant for edibility. Some plants have both edible and inedible parts. **NEVER ASSUME** a part that proved edible when cooked is edible raw, test the part raw before eating . The same part or plant may produce varying reactions in different individuals.

(1) Test only 1 part of a plant at a time.
(2) Separate the plant into its basic components (stems, roots, buds, and flowers).
(3) Smell the food for strong acid odors. Remember, smell alone does not indicate a plant is edible or inedible.
(4) *DO NOT* eat 8 hours before the test and drink only purified water.
(5) During the 8 hours you abstain from eating, test for contact poisoning by placing a piece of the plant on the inside of your elbow or wrist. The sap or juice should contact the skin. Usually 15 minutes is enough time to allow for a reaction.
(6) During testing, take *NOTHING* by mouth **EXCEPT** purified water and the plant you are testing.
(7) Select a small portion of a single part and prepare it the way you plan to eat it.
(8) Before placing the prepared plant in your mouth, touch a small portion (a pinch) to the outer surface of your lip to test for burning or itching.

(9)  If after 3 minutes there is no reaction on your lip, place the plant on your tongue and hold it for 15 minutes.

(10) If there is no reaction, thoroughly chew a pinch and hold it in your mouth for 15 minutes (*DO NOT SWALLOW*). If any ill effects occur, rinse out your mouth with water.

(11) If nothing abnormal occurs, swallow the food and wait 8 hours. **If any illeffects** occur during this period, **induce** vomiting and drink a water and charcoal mixture.

(12) If no ill effects occur, eat ¼ **cup** of the same plant prepared the same way. Wait another 8 hours. If no ill effects occur, the plant part as prepared is safe for eating.

**CAUTION:** 1. Ripe tropical fruits should be peeled and eaten raw. Softness, rather than color, is the best indicator of ripeness. Cook unripe fruits and discard seeds and skin.

2. Cook underground portions when possible to reduce bacterial contamination and ease digestion of their generally high starch content.

3. During evaluation, you may not be able to cook. Concentrate your efforts on leafy green plants, ripe fruits, and above ground ripe vegetables not requiring signification preparation.

## 2. FOOD PREPARATION
Animal food gives the greatest food value per pound.
### A.  BUTCHERING AND SKINNING.
(1)  Mammals.
(a)  Remove the skin and save for other uses.
(a)  One cut skinning of small game.
- Open the abdominal cavity.
- Avoid rupturing the intestines.
- Remove the intestines.
- Save inner organs (heart, liver, and kidneys) and all meaty parts of the skull, brain, tongue, and eyes.
(b)  Wash when ready to use.
(c)  If preserving the meat, remove it from the bones.
(d)  Unused or inedible organs and entrails may be used as bait for other game.

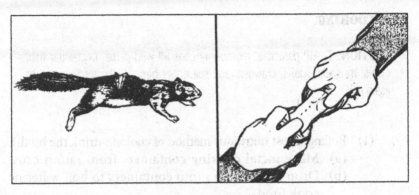

**Small Game Skinning**

(2) Frogs and snakes.
- (a) Skin.
- (b) Discard skin, head with 2 inches of body, and internal organs.

(3) Fish.
- (a) Scale (if necessary) and gut fish soon after it is caught.
- (b) Insert knifepoint into anus of fish and cut open the belly.
- (c) Remove entrails.
- (d) Remove gills to prevent spoilage.

(4) Birds.
- (a) Gut soon after killing.
- (b) Protect from flies.
- (c) Skin or pluck them.
- (d) Skin scavengers and sea birds.

(5) Insects.
- (a) Remove all hard portions such as the legs of grasshoppers or crickets. (The rest is edible.)
- (b) Recommend cooking grasshopper-size insects.

**CAUTION:** Dead insects spoil rapidly, **DO NOT** save.

(6) Fruits, berries, and most nuts can be eaten raw.

## B. COOKING.

> **CAUTION:** To kill parasites, thoroughly cook all wild game, freshwater fish, clams, mussels, snails, crawfish, and scavenger birds. Saltwater fish may be eaten raw.

    (1) Boiling (most nutritious method of cooking-drink the broth).
        (a) Make metal cooking containers from ration cans.
        (b) Drop heated rocks into containers to boil water or cook food.
    (2) Baking.
        (a) Wrap in leaves or pack in mud.
        (b) Bury food in dirt under coals of fire.
    (3) Leaching. Some nuts (acorns) must be leached to remove the bitter taste of tannin. Use one of the following leaching methods:
        (a) First method:
            • Soaking and pouring the water off.
            • Crushing and pouring water through. Cold water should be tried first; however, boiling water is sometimes best.
            • Discarding water.
        (b) Second method:
            • Boil, pour off water, and taste the plant.
            • If bitter, repeat process until palatable.
    (4) Roasting.
        (a) Shake shelled nuts in a container with hot coals.
        (b) Roast thinly sliced meat and insects over a candle.

## 3. FOOD PRESERVATION

  b. Keeping an animal alive.
  c. Refrigerating.
    (1) Long term.
        (a) Food buried in snow maintains a temperature of approximately 32 degrees F.
        (b) Frozen food will not decompose (freeze in meal-size portions).

(2) Short term.

    (a) Food wrapped in waterproof material and placed in a stream remains cool in summer months.

    (b) Earth below the surface, particularly in shady areas or along streams, is cooler than the surface.

    (c) Wrap food in absorbent material such as cotton and re-wet as the water evaporates.

c. Drying and smoking removes moisture and preserves food.

    (1) Use salt to improve flavor and promote drying.

    (2) Cut or pound meat into thin strips.

    (3) Remove fat.

    (4) *DO NOT* use pitch woods such as fir or pine; they produce soot giving the meat an undesirable taste.

d. Protecting meat from animals and insects.

    (1) Wrapping food.

        (a) Use clean material.

        (b) Wrap pieces individually.

        (c) Ensure all corners of the wrapping are insect proof.

        (d) Wrap soft fruits and berries in leaves or moss.

    (2) Hanging meat.

        (a) Hang meat in the shade.

        (b) Cover during daylight hours to protect from insects.

    (3) Packing meat on the trail.

        (a) Wrap before flies appear in the morning.

        (b) Place meat in fabric or clothing for insulation.

        (c) Place meat inside the pack for carrYing. Soft material acts as insulation helping keep the meat cool.

        (d) Carry shellfish, crabs, and shrimp in wet seaweed.

e. *DO NOT* store food in the shelter; it attracts unwanted animals.

## CHAPTER 8

# FIRECRAFT

In many survival situations, the ability to start a fire can make the difference between living and dying. Fire can fulfill many needs. It can provide warmth and comfort. It not only cooks and preserves food, but it also provides warmth in the form of heated food that saves calories your body normally uses to produce body heat. You can use fire to purify water, sterilize bandages, signal for rescue, and provide protection from animals. It can be a psychological boost by providing peace of mind and companionship. You can also use fire to produce tools and weapons.

Fire can cause problems, as well. It can cause forest fires or destroy essential equipment. Fire can also cause burns and carbon monoxide poisoning when used in shelters.

## BASIC FIRE PRINCIPLES

To build a fire, it helps to understand the basic principles of a fire. Fuel (in a nongaseous state) does not burn directly. When you apply heat to a fuel, it produces a gas. This gas, combined with oxygen in the air, burns.

Understanding the concept of the fire triangle is very important in correctly constructing and maintaining a fire. The three sides of the triangle represent *air, heat,* and *fuel.* If you remove any of these, the fire will go out. The correct ratio of these components is very important for a fire to burn at its greatest capability. The only way to learn this ratio is to practice.

# SITE SELECTION AND PREPARATION

You will have to decide what site and arrangement to use. Before building a fire, consider:

- The area (terrain and climate) in which you are operating.
- The materials and tools available.
- How much time you have?
- Why do you need a fire?
- Look for a dry spot that:
  - Is protected from the wind.
  - Is suitably placed in relation to your shelter (if any).
  - Will concentrate the heat in the direction you desire.
  - Has a supply of wood or other fuel available. (See page 7-6 for types of material you can use.)

If you are in a wooded or brush-covered area, clear the brush and scrape the surface soil from the spot you have selected. Clear a circle at least 1 meter in diameter so there is little chance of the fire spreading. If time allows, construct a fire wall using logs or rocks. This wall will help to reflect or direct the heat where you want it (Figure 8-1). It will also reduce flying sparks and cut down on the amount of wind blowing into the fire. However, you will need enough wind to keep the fire burning.

**CAUTION**
Do not use wet or porous rocks as they may explode when heated.

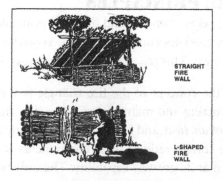

**Types of fire walls**

In some situations, you may find that an underground fireplace will best meet your needs. It conceals the fire and serves well for cooking food. To make an underground fireplace or Dakota fire hole:

- Dig a hole in the ground.
- On the upwind side of this hole, poke or dig a large connecting hole for ventilation.
- Build your fire in the hole as illustrated.

If you are in a snow-covered area, use green logs to make a dry base for your fire. Trees with wrist-sized trunks are easily broken in extreme cold. Cut or break several green logs and lay them side by side on top of the snow. Add one or two more layers. Lay the top layer of logs opposite those below it.

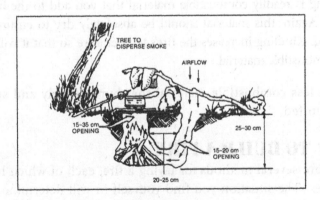

Dakota fire hole.

Base for fire in snow-covered area.

# FIRE MATERIAL SELECTION

You need three types of materials to build a fire—tinder, kindling, and fuel.

Tinder is dry material that ignites with little heat—a spark starts a fire. The tinder must be absolutely dry to be sure just a spark will ignite it. If you only have a device that generates sparks, charred cloth will be almost essential. It holds a spark for long periods, allowing you to put tinder on the hot area to generate a small flame. You can make charred cloth by heating cotton cloth until it turns black, but does not burn. Once it is black, you must keep it in an airtight container to keep it dry. Prepare this cloth well in advance of any survival situation. Add it to your individual survival kit.

Kindling is readily combustible material that you add to the burning tinder. Again, this material should be absolutely dry to ensure rapid burning. Kindling increases the fire's temperature so that it will ignite less combustible material.

Fuel is less combustible material that burns slowly and steadily once ignited.

# HOW TO BUILD A FIRE

There are several methods for laying a fire, each of which has advantages. The situation you find yourself in will determine which fire to use.

## TEPEE

To make this fire, arrange the tinder and a few sticks of kindling in the shape of a tepee or cone. Light the center. As the tepee burns, the outside logs will fall inward, feeding the fire. This type of fire burns well even with wet wood.

## LEAN-TO

To lay this fire, push a green stick into the ground at a 30-degree angle. Point the end of the stick in the direction of the wind. Place some tinder deep under this lean-to stick. Lean pieces of kindling against the lean-to stick. Light the tinder. As the kindling catches fire from the tinder, add more kindling.

| Tinder | Kindling | Fuel |
|---|---|---|
| • Birch bark<br>• Shredded inner bark from cedar, chestnut, red elm trees<br>• Fine wood shavings<br>• Dead grass, ferns, moss, fungi<br>• Straw<br>• Sawdust<br>• Very fine pitchwood scrapings<br>• Dead evergreen needles<br>• Punk (the completely rotted portions of dead logs or trees)<br>• Evergreen tree knots<br>• Bird down (fine feathers)<br>• Down seed heads (milkweed, dry cattails, bulrush, or thistle)<br>• Fine, dried vegetable fibers<br>• Spongy threads of dead puffball<br>• Dead palm leaves<br>• Skinlike membrane lining bamboo<br>• Lint from pocket and seams<br>• Charred cloth<br>• Waxed paper<br>• Outer bamboo shavings<br>• Gunpowder<br>• Cotton<br>• Lint | • Small twigs<br>• Small strips of wood<br>• Split wood<br>• Heavy cardboard<br>• Pieces of wood removed from the inside of larger pieces<br>• Wood that has been doused with highly flammable materials, such as gasoline, oil or wax | • Dry, standing wood and dry, dead branches<br>• Dry inside (heart) of fallen tree trunks and large branches<br>• Green wood that is finely split<br>• Dry grasses twisted into bunches<br>• Peat dry enough to burn (this may be found at the top of undercut banks)<br>• Dried animal dung<br>• Animal fats<br>• Coal, oil shale, or oil lying on the surface |

**Materials for building fires.**

## CROSS-DITCH

To use this method, scratch a cross about 12 inches in size in the ground. Dig the cross 3 inches deep. Put a large wad of tinder in the middle of the cross. Build a kindling pyramid above the tinder. The shallow ditch allows air to sweep under the tinder to provide a draft.

## PYRAMID

To lay this fire, place two small logs or branches parallel on the ground. Place a solid layer of small logs across the parallel logs. Add three or four more layers of logs or branches, each layer smaller than and at a right angle to the layer below it. Make a starter fire on top of the pyramid. As the starter fire burns, it will ignite the logs below it. This gives you a fire that burns downward, requiring no attention during the night.

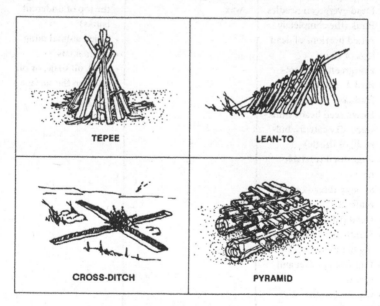

Methods for laying fires.

There are several other ways to lay a fire that are quite effective. Your situation and the material available in the area may make another method more suitable.

# HOW TO LIGHT A FIRE

Always light your fire from the upwind side. Make sure to lay your tinder, kindling, and fuel so that your fire will burn as long as you need it. Igniters provide the initial heat required to start the tinder burning. They fall into two categories: modem methods and primitive methods.

## MODERN METHODS

Modem igniters use modem devices—items we normally think of to start a fire.

### Matches

Make sure these matches are waterproof. Also, store them in a waterproof container along with a dependable striker pad.

### Convex Lens

Use this method (Figure 8-6) only on bright, sunny days. The lens can come from binoculars, camera, telescopic sights, or magnifying glasses. Angle the lens to concentrate the sun's rays on the tinder. Hold the lens over the same spot until the tinder begins to smolder. Gently blow or fan the tinder into flame, and apply it to the fire lay.

### Metal Match

Place a flat, dry leaf under your tinder with a portion exposed. Place the tip of the metal match on the dry leaf, holding the metal match in one hand and a knife in the other. Scrape your knife against the metal match to produce sparks. The sparks will hit the tinder. When the tinder starts to smolder, proceed as above.

### Battery

Use a battery to generate a spark. Use of this method depends on the type of battery available. Attach a wire to each terminal. Touch the ends of the bare wires together next to the tinder so the sparks will ignite it.

### Gunpowder

If you have ammunition with you, carefully extract the bullet from the shell casing, and use the gunpowder as tinder. A spark will ignite the powder. Be extremely careful when extracting the bullet from the case.

## PRIMITIVE METHODS

Primitive igniters are those attributed to our early ancestors.

### Flint and Steel

The direct spark method is the easiest of the primitive methods to use. The flint and steel method is the most reliable of the direct spark methods. Strike a flint or other hard, sharp-edged rock edge with a piece of carbon steel (stainless steel will not produce a good spark). This method requires a loose-jointed wrist and practice. When a spark has caught in the tinder, blow on it. The spark will spread and burst into flames.

### Fire-Plow

The fire-plow is a friction method of ignition. You rub a hardwood shaft against a softer wood base. To use this method, cut a straight groove in the base and plow the blunt tip of the shaft up and down the groove. The plowing action of the shaft pushes out small particles of wood fibers. Then, as you apply more pressure on each stroke, the friction ignites the wood particles.

Lens method.

### Bow and Drill

The technique of starting a fire with a bow and drill (Figure 8-8) is simple, but you must exert much effort and be persistent to produce a fire. You need the following items to use this method:

- Socket. The socket is an easily grasped stone or piece of hardwood or bone with a slight depression in one side. Use it to hold the drill in place and to apply downward pressure.
- Drill. The drill should be a straight, seasoned hardwood stick about 2 centimeters in diameter and 25 centimeters long. The top end is round and the low end blunt (to produce more friction).
- Fire board. Its size is up to you. A seasoned softwood board about

2.5 centimeters thick and 10 centimeters wide is preferable. Cut a depression about 2 centimeters from the edge on one side of the board. On the underside, make a V-shaped cut from the edge of the board to the depression.

- *Bow.* The bow is a resilient, green stick about 2.5 centimeters in diameter and a string. The type of wood is not important. The bowstring can be any type of cordage. You tie the bowstring from one end of the bow to the other, without any slack.

To use the bow and drill, first prepare the fire lay. Then place a bundle of tinder under the V-shaped cut in the fire board. Place one foot on the fire board. Loop the bowstring over the drill and place the drill in the precut depression on the fire board. Place the socket, held in one hand, on the top of the drill to hold it in position. Press down on the drill and saw the bow back and forth to twirl the drill. Once you have established a smooth motion, apply more downward pressure and work the bow faster. This action will grind hot black powder into the tinder, causing a spark to catch. Blow on the tinder until it ignites.

Fire-plow.

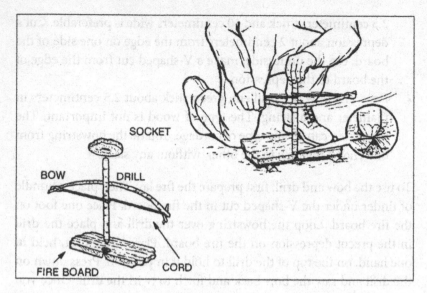

**Bow and drill.**

*Note: Primitive fire-building methods are exhaustive and require practice to ensure success.*

### HELPFUL HINTS

Use nonaromatic seasoned hardwood for fuel, if possible.

Collect kindling and tinder along the trail.

Add insect repellent to the tinder.

Keep the firewood dry.

Dry damp firewood near the fire.

Bank the fire to keep the coals alive overnight,

Carry lighted punk, when possible.

Be sure the fire is out before leaving camp.

Do not select wood lying on the ground. It may appear to be dry but generally doesn't provide enough friction.

## CHAPTER 9

# MEDICAL

**WARNING:** These emergency medical procedures are for survival situations. Obtain professional medical treatment as soon as possible.

## 1. IMMEDIATE FIRST AID ACTIONS

**Remember the *ABCs* of Emergency care:**

Airway          Breating          Circulation

a. Determine responsiveness as follows:
  (1) If unconscious, arouse by shaking gently and shouting.
  (2) If no response—
    (a) Keep head and neck aligned with body.
    (b) Roll victims onto their backs.
    (c) Open the airway by lifting the chin.
    (d) Look, listen, and feel for air exchange.
  (3) If victim is not breathing—
    (a) Check for a clear airway; remove any blockage.
    (b) Cover victim's mouth with your own.
    (c) Pinch victim's nostrils closed.
    (d) Fill victim's lungs with 2 slow breaths.
    (e) If breaths are blocked, reposition airway; try again.
    (f) If breaths still blocked, give **5** abdominal thrusts:

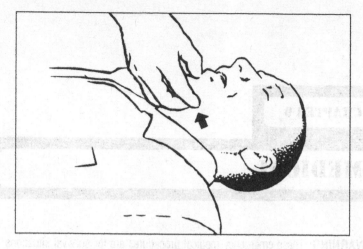

**Chin Lift**

- Straddle the victim.
- Place a fist between breastbone and belly button.
- Thrust upward to expel air from stomach
(g) Sweep with finger to clear mouth,
(h) Try **2** slow breaths again.
(i) If the airway is still blocked, continue (c) through (f) until successful or exhausted.
(j) With open airway, start mouth to mouth breathing:
  - Give **1** breath every 5 seconds.
  - Check for chest rise each time.
(4) If victim is unconscious, but breathing—
  (a) Keep head and neck aligned with body.
  (b) Roll victim on side (drains the mouth and prevents the tongue from blocking airway).

**CAUTION:** ***DO NOT*** remove an impaled object unless it interferes with the airway. You may cause more tissue damage and increase bleeding. For travel, you may shorten and secure the object.

b. Control bleeding as follows:
  (1) Apply a pressure dressing.
  (2) If *STILL* bleeding—
    (a) Use direct pressure over the wound.
    (b) Elevate the wounded area above the heart.

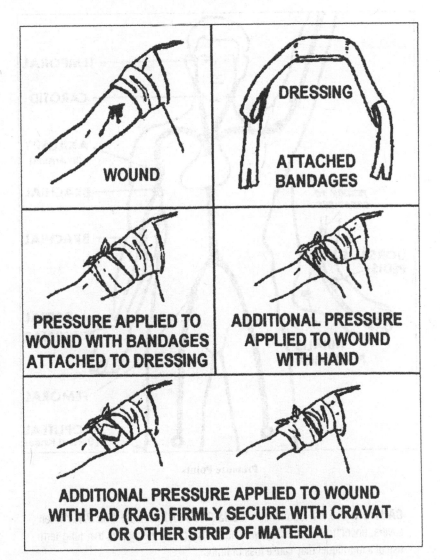

**WOUND**

**DRESSING**

**ATTACHED BANDAGES**

**PRESSURE APPLIED TO WOUND WITH BANDAGES ATTACHED TO DRESSING**

**ADDITIONAL PRESSURE APPLIED TO WOUND WITH HAND**

**ADDITIONAL PRESSURE APPLIED TO WOUND WITH PAD (RAG) FIRMLY SECURE WITH CRAVAT OR OTHER STRIP OF MATERIAL**

Application of a Pressure Dressing

(3) If *STILL* bleeding—

    (a) Use a pressure point between the injury and the heart.

    (b) Maintain pressure for 6 to 10 minutes before checking to see if bleeding has stopped.

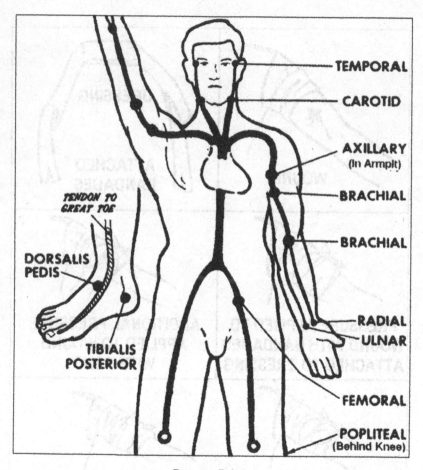

**Pressure Points**

**CAUTION:** Use of a tourniquet is a *LAST RESORT* measure. Use *ONLY* when severe, uncontrolled bleeding will cause loss of life. Recognize that long-term use of a tourniquet may cause loss of limb.

(4) If a limb wound is *STILL* bleeding—
  (a) Apply tourniquet (TK) band just above bleeding site on limb. A band at least 3 inches (7.5 cm) or wider is best.
  (b) Follow steps illustrated on page 80.
  (c) Use a stick at least 6 inches (15 cm) long.
  (d) Tighten only enough to stop arterial bleeding.
  (e) Mark a *TK* on the forehead with the time applied.
  (f) *DO NOT* cover the tourniquet.

**CAUTION:** The following directions apply *ONLY* in survival situations where rescue is *UNLIKELY* and *NO* medical aid is available.

  (g) If rescue or medical aid is not available for over 2 hours, an attempt to *SLOWLY* loosen the tourniquet may be made 20 minutes after application. Before loosening—
    • Ensure pressure dressing is in place.
    • Ensure bleeding has stopped
    • Loosen tourniquet *SLOWLY* to restore circulation.
    • Leave loosened tourniquet in position in case bleeding resumes.

c. Treat shock. (Shock is difficult to identify or treat under field conditions. It may be present with or without visible injury.)
  (1) Identify by one or more of the following:
    (a) Pale, cool, and sweaty skin.
    (b) Fast breathing and a weak, fast pulse.
    (c) Anxiety or mental confusion.
    (d) Decreased urine output.
  (2) Maintain circulation.
  (3) Treat underlying injury.
  (4) Maintain normal body temperature.
    (a) Remove wet clothing.
    (b) Give warm fluids.
      • *DO NOT* give fluids to an unconscious victim.
      • *DO NOT* give fluids if they cause victim to gag.

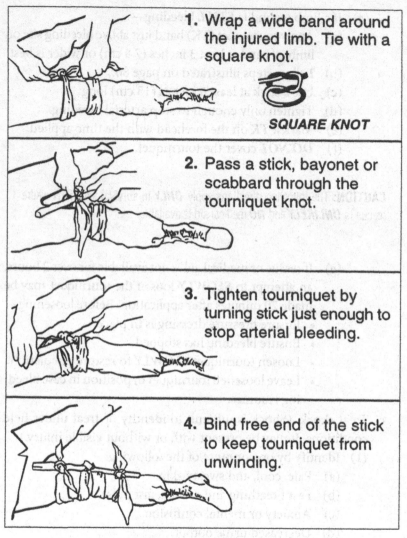

1. Wrap a wide band around the injured limb. Tie with a square knot.

**SQUARE KNOT**

2. Pass a stick, bayonet or scabbard through the tourniquet knot.

3. Tighten tourniquet by turning stick just enough to stop arterial bleeding.

4. Bind free end of the stick to keep tourniquet from unwinding.

**Application of a Tourniquet**

    (c)   Insulate from ground.

    (d)   Shelter from the elements.

(5)  Place conscious victim on back.

(6)  Place very weak or unconscious victim on side, this will—

    (a)   Allow mouth to drain.

    (b)   Prevent tongue from blocking airway.

d. Treat chest injuries.

  (1) Sucking chest wound. This occurs when chest wall is penetrated; may cause victim to gasp for breath; may cause sucking sound; may create bloody froth as air escapes the chest.

    (a) *Immediately* seal wound with hand or airtight material.

    (b) Tape airtight material over wound on *3 sides only* to allow air to escape from the wound but not to enter.

    (c) Monitor breathing and check dressing.

    (d) Lift untapped side of dressing as victim *exhales* to allow trapped air to escape, as necessary.

  (2) Flail chest. Results from blunt trauma when *3* or *more* ribs are broken in *2* or more places. The flail segment is the broken area that moves in a direction opposite to the rest of chest during breathing.

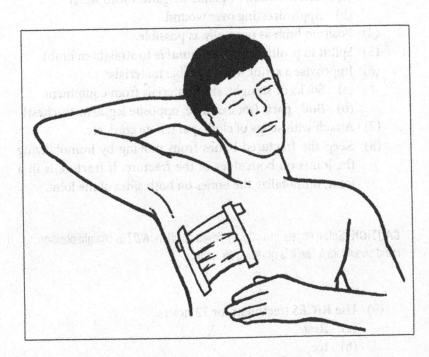

**Sucking Chest Wound Dressing**

      (a)  Stabilize the flail segment as follows:
- Place rolled-up clothing or bulky pad over site.
- Tape pad to site
- *DO NOT* wrap tape around chest.

      (b)  Have victim keep segment still with hand pressure.

      (c)  Roll victim onto side of flail segment injury (as other injuries allow).

  (3)  Fractured ribs.

      (a)  Encourage deep breathing (painful, but necessary to prevent the possible development of pneumonia).

      (b)  *DO NOT* constrict breathing by taping ribs.

e.  Treat fractures, sprains, and dislocations.

  (1)  Control bleeding.

  (2)  Remove watches, jewelry, and constrictive clothing.

  (3)  If fracture penetrates the skin—

      (a)  Clean wound by gentle irrigation with water.

      (b)  Apply dressing over wound.

  (4)  Position limb as normally as possible.

  (5)  Splint in position found (if *unable* to straighten limb).

  (6)  Improvise a splint with available materials:

      (a)  Sticks or straight, stiff materials from equipment.

      (b)  Body parts (for example, opposite leg, arm-to-chest).

  (7)  Attach with strips of cloth, parachute cord, etc.

  (8)  Keep the fractured bones from moving by immobilizing the joints on both sides of the fracture. If fracture is in a joint, immobilize the bones on both sides of the joint.

---

**CAUTION:** Splint fingers in a slightly flexed position, *NOT* in straight position. Hand should look like it is grasping an apple.

---

  (9)  Use *RICES* treatment for 72 hours.

      (a)  Rest.

      (b)  Ice.

      (c)  Compression.

(d) Elevation.

(e) Stabilization.

(10) Apply cold to acute injuries.

(11) Use 15 to 20 minute periods of cold application.

    (a) *DO NOT* use continuous cold therapy.

    (b) Repeat 3 to 4 times per day.

    (c) Avoid cooling that can cause frostbite or hypothermia.

(12) Wrap with a compression bandage after cold therapy.

(13) Elevate injured area above heart level to reduce swelling.

(14) Check periodically for a pulse beyond the injury site.

(15) Loosen bandage or reapply splint if no pulse is felt or if swelling occurs because bandage is too tight.

## 2. COMMON INJURIES AND ILLNESSES

a. Burns.

    (1) Cool the burned area with water.

        (a) Use immersion or cool compresses.

        (b) Avoid aggressive cooling with ice or frigid water.

    (2) Remove watches, jewelry, constrictive clothing.

    (3) *DO NOT* remove embedded, charred material that will cause burned areas to bleed.

    (4) Cover with sterile dressings.

    (5) *DO NOT* use lotion or grease.

    (6) Avoid moving or rubbing the burned part.

    (7) Drink *extra* water to compensate for increased fluid loss from burns. (Add ¼ *teaspoon* of *salt* [if available] to *each quart* of *water*.)

    (8) Change dressings when soaked or dirty.

b. Eye injuries.

    (1) Sun/snow blindness (gritty, burning sensation, and possible reduction in vision caused by sun exposure).

        (a) Prevent with improvised goggles.

        (b) Treat by patching affected eye(s).

            • Check after 12 hours.

            • Replace patch for another 12 hours if not healed.

        (c) Use cool compresses to reduce pain.

(2) Foreign body in eye.
   (a) Irrigate with clean water from the *inside* to the *outside* corner of the eye.
   (b) If foreign body is not removed by irrigation, improvise a small swab. Moisten and wipe gently over the affected area.
   (c) If foreign body is *STILL* not removed, patch eye for 24 hours and then reattempt removal using steps (a) and (b).

c. Heat injury.
  (1) Heat cramps (cramps in legs or abdomen).
   (a) Rest.
   (b) Drink water. Add ¼ *teaspoon* of salt *per quart.*
  (2) Heat exhaustion (pale, sweating, moist, cool skin).
   (a) Rest in shade.
   (b) Drink water.
   (c) Protect from further heat exposure.
  (3) Heat stroke (victim disoriented or unconscious, skin is hot and flushed [sweating **may** or **may not** occur], fast pulse).

> **CAUTION:** Handle heat stroke victim gently. Shock, seizures, and cardiac arrest can occur.

   (a) Cool as rapidly as possible (saturate clothing with water and fan the victim). Remember to cool the groin and armpit areas. (Avoid overcooling.)
   (b) Maintain airway, breathing, and circulation.

d. Cold injuries:
  (1) Frostnip and frostbite—
   (a) Are progressive injuries.
    • Ears, nose, fingers, and toes are affected first.
    • Areas will feel cold and may tingle leading to—
     ••Numbness that progresses to—
      ••• Waxy appearance with stiff skin that cannot glide freely over a joint.

(b) Frostnipped areas rewarm with body heat. If body heat **WILL NOT** rewarm area in 15 to 20 minutes, then frostbite is present.

(c) Frostbitten areas are deeply frozen and require medical treatment.

**CAUTION:** In frostbite, repeated freezing and thawing causes severe pain and increases damage to the tissue. **DO NOT** rub frozen tissue. **DO NOT** thaw frozen tissue.

(2) Hypothermia—
   (a) Is a progressive injury.
   - Intense shivering with impaired ability to perform complex tasks leads to—
     •• Violent shivering, difficulty speaking, sluggish thinking go to—
       ••• Muscular rigidity with blue, puffy skin; jerky movements go to—
         ••••Coma, respiratory and cardiac failure.
   (b) Protect victim from the environment as follows:
   - Remove wet clothing.
   - Put on dry clothing (if available).
   - Prevent further heat loss.
     ••Cover top of head.
     ••Insulate from above and below.
   - Warm with blankets, sleeping bags, or shelter.
   - Warm central areas before extremities.
     ••Place heat packs in groin, armpits, and around neck.
     ••Avoid causing burns to skin.

**CAUTION:** Handle hypothermia victim gently. Avoid overly rapid rewarming which may cause cardiac arrest. Rewarming of victim with skin-to-skin contact by volunteer(s) inside of a sleeping bag is a survival technique but can cause internal temperatures of all to drop.

e. Skin tissue damage.

   (1) Immersion injuries. Skin becomes wrinkled as in *dishpan hands.*

     (a) Avoid walking on affected feet.

     (b) Pat dry; *DO NOT* rub. Skin tissue will be sensitive.

     (c) Dry socks and shoes. Keep feet protected.

     (d) Loosen boots, cuffs, etc., to improve circulation.

     (e) Keep area dry, warm, and open to air.

     (f) *DO NOT* apply creams or ointments.

   (2) Saltwater sores.

     (a) Change body positions frequently.

     (b) Keep sores dry.

     (c) Use antiseptic (if available).

     (d) *DO NOT* open or squeeze sores.

f. Snakebite.

**CAUTION:** This snakebite treatment recommendation is for situations where medical aid and specialized equipment are not available.

   (1) Nonpoisonous. Clean and bandage wound.

   (2) Poisonous.

     (a) Remove constricting items.

     (b) Minimize activity.

     (c) *DO NOT* cut the bite site; *DO NOT* use your mouth to create suction.

     (d) Clean bite with soap and water; cover with a dressing.

     (e) Overwrap the bite site with a tight (elastic) bandage **(Figure V-6)**. The intent is to slow capillary and venous blood flow but not arterial flow. Check for pulse below the overwrap.

     (f) Splint bitten extremity to prevent motion.

     (g) Treat for shock.

     (h) Position extremity below level of heart.

     (i) Construct shelter if necessary (let the victim rest).

(j) For conscious victims, force fluids.

g. Marine life.

(1) Stings.

(a) Flush wound with salt water (fresh water stimulates toxin release).

(b) Remove jewelry and watches.

(c) Remove tentacles and gently scrape or shave skin.

(d) Apply a steroid cream (if available).

(e) **DO NOT** rub area with sand.

(f) Treat for shock; artificial respiration may be required.

(g) **DO NOT** use urine to flush or treat wounds.

(2) Punctures.

(a) Immerse affected part in hot water or apply hot compresses for 30-60 minutes (as hot as victim can tolerate).

(b) Cover with clean dressing.

(c) Treat for shock as needed.

h. Skin irritants (includes poison oak and poison ivy).

(1) Wash with large amounts of water. Use soap (if available).

(2) Keep covered to prevent scratching,

i. Infection.

(1) Keep wound clean.

(2) Use iodine tablet solution or diluted betadine to prevent or treat infection.

(3) Change bandages as needed.

j. Dysentery and diarrhea.

(1) Drink *extra* water.

(2) Use a liquid diet.

(3) Eat charcoal. Make a paste by mixing fine charcoal particles with water. (It may relieve symptoms by absorbing toxins.)

k. Constipation (can be expected in survival situations).

(1) **DO NOT** take laxatives.

(2) Exercise.

(3) Drink *extra* water.

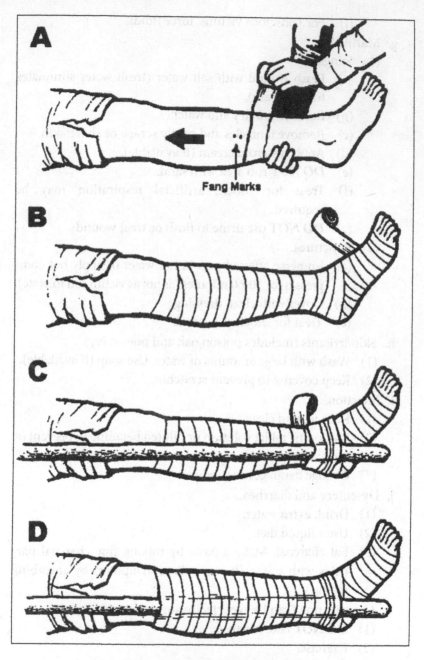

Fang Marks

Compression Bandage for Snake Bite

# 3. PLANT MEDICINE

a. Tannin.

  (1) Medical uses. Burns, diarrhea, dysentery, skin problems, and parasites. Tannin solution prevents infection and aids healing.

  (2) Sources. Found in the outer bark of all trees, acorns, banana plants, common plantain, strawberry leaves, and blackberry stems.

  (3) Preparation.

    (a) Place crushed outer bark, acorns, or leaves in water.

    (b) Leach out the tannin by soaking or boiling.

      • Increase tannin content by longer soaking time.

      • Replace depleted material with fresh bark/plants.

  (4) Treatments.

    (a) Burns.

      • Moisten bandage with cooled tannin tea.

      • Apply compress to burned area.

      • Pour cooled tea on burned areas to ease pain.

    (b) Diarrhea, dysentery, and worms. Drink strong tea solution (may promote voiding of worms).

    (c) Skin problems (dry rashes and fungal infections). Apply cool compresses or soak affected part to relieve itching and promote healing.

    (d) Lice and insect bites. Wash affected areas with tea to ease itching.

b. Salicin/salicylic acid.

  (1) Medical uses. Aches, colds, fever, inflammation, pain, sprains, and sore throat (aspirin-like qualities).

  (2) Sources. Willow and aspen trees.

  (3) Preparation.

    (a) Gather twigs, buds, or cambium layer (soft, moist layer between the outer bark and the wood) of willow or aspen.

    (b) Prepare tea.

    (c) Make poultice.

- Crush the plant or stems.
- Make a pulpy mass.

(4) Treatments.

    (a) Chew on twigs, buds, or cambium for symptom relief.

    (b) Drink tea for colds and sore throat.

    (c) Use warm, moist poultice for aches and sprains.

- Apply pulpy mass over injury.
- Hold in place with a dressing.

c. Common plantain

  (1) Medical uses. Itching, wounds, abrasions, stings, diarrhea, and dysentery.

  (2) Source. There are over 200 plantain species with similar medicinal properties.

  (3) Preparation.

    (a) Brew tea from seeds.

    (b) Brew tea from leaves.

    (c) Make poultice of leaves.

  (4) Treatments.

    (a) Drink tea made from seeds for diarrhea or dysentery.

    (b) Drink tea made from leaves for vitamin and minerals.

    (c) Use poultice to treat cuts, sores, burns, and stings.

d. Papain.

  (1) Medical uses. Digestive aid, meat tenderizer, and a food source.

  (2) Source. Fruit of the papaya tree.

  (3) Preparation.

    (a) Make cuts in **unripe** fruit.

    (b) Gather milky white sap for its papain content.

    (c) Avoid getting sap in eyes or wounds.

  (4) Treatments.

    (a) Use sap to tenderize tough meat.

    (b) Eat **ripe** fruit for food, vitamins, and minerals.

e. Common Cattail.

  (1) Medical uses. Wounds, sores, boils, inflammations, burns, and an excellent food source.

   (2)  Source. Cattail plant found in marshes.
   (3)  Preparation.
       (a)  Pound roots into a pulpy mass for a poultice.
       (b)  Cook and eat green bloom spikes.
       (c)  Collect yellow pollen for flour substitute.
       (d)  Peel and eat tender shoots (raw or cooked).
   (4)  Treatments.
       (a)  Apply poultice to affected area.
       (b)  Use plant for food, vitamins, and minerals.

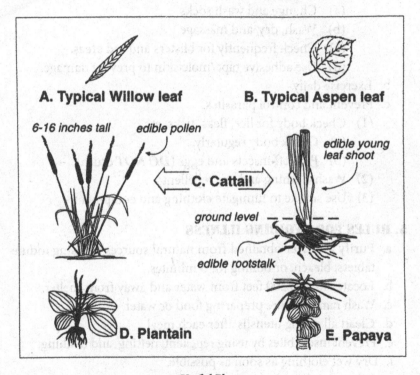

**A. Typical Willow leaf**

**B. Typical Aspen leaf**

*6-16 inches tall*    *edible pollen*

*edible young leaf shoot*

**C. Cattail**

*ground level*

*edible rootstalk*

**D. Plantain**

**E. Papaya**

**Useful Plants**

## 4. HEALTH AND HYGIENE

  a. Stay clean (daily regimen).
     (1)  Minimize infection by washing. (Use white ashes, sand, or loamy soil as soap substitutes.)
     (2)  Comb and clean debris from hair.

(3) Cleanse mouth and brush teeth.
    (a) Use hardwood twig as toothbrush (fray it by chewing on one end then use as brush).
    (b) Use single strand of an inner core string from parachute cord for dental floss.
    (c) Use clean finger to stimulate gum tissues by rubbing.
    (d) Gargle with salt water to help prevent sore throat and aid in cleaning teeth and gums.
(4) Clean and protect feet.
    (a) Change and wash socks
    (b) Wash, dry, and massage.
    (c) Check frequently for blisters and red areas.
    (d) Use adhesive tape/mole skin to prevent damage.

b. Exercise daily.

c. Prevent and control parasites.
    (1) Check body for lice, fleas, ticks, etc.
        (a) Check body regularly.
        (b) Pick off insects and eggs (**DO NOT** crush).
    (2) Wash clothing and use repellents.
    (3) Use smoke to fumigate clothing and equipment.

## 5. RULES FOR AVOIDING ILLNESS

a. Purify all water obtained from natural sources by using iodine tablets, bleach, or boiling for 5 minutes.

b. Locate latrines 200 feet from water and away from shelter.

c. Wash hands before preparing food or water.

d. Clean all eating utensils after each meal.

e. Prevent insect bites by using repellent, netting, and clothing.

f. Dry wet clothing as soon as possible.

g. Eat varied diet.

h. Try to get 7-8 hours sleep per day.

## CHAPTER 10

# SURVIVAL SHELTERS

A careful assessment of the survival situation in which you find yourself will make it possible to decide on an order of priorities. One of the key decisions you will have to make is where the need for shelter lies within that order. In most survival situations finding shelter will be a matter of urgency. Even in a temperate part of the world it will usually be a need that you cannot afford to overlook.

The most dangerous weather conditions include cold, wind, rain and snow. It is essential to protect yourself against these, as each of them is a factor which brings about hypothermia—a drop in the body temperature below the normal level. Exposure to one or any combination of these conditions can rapidly produce deadly results long before any shortage of food or water would take effect. Conversely, even in warm summer weather or hot climates, shelter from the sun is needed in order to avoid overheating of the body. Prolonged exposure to high temperatures may not effect the survivor as quickly as loss of body heat, but it can still have fatal consequences by causing a very rapid loss of body fluids.

## CHOOSING A SITE

There may be temporary shelter to be found among the natural features immediately surrounding you or nearby. Seek it in or near trees, thick bushes or natural hollows. If on close inspection they seem safe, make use of caves, rock overhangs or any stable form of natural shelter. Never waste precious time and energy constructing a temporary shelter or wind-break if nature already provides it.

The climate and the terrain, along with your personal circumstances—for example, whether you are alone or in a group, the physical condition you are in, and the construction materials and tools you have at your disposal—will to a large extent determine

**Find cover as quickly as possible. Take into account your state of health and any construction tools available. The most important considerations are insulation from the ground and protection from the weather. Don't attempt to build anything too complicated until you have the time.**

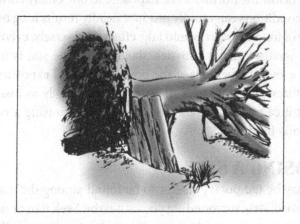

**A natural shelter, such as this fallen tree, can be easily improved with logs acting as a windbreak. It is most important to settle on your shelter before the cover of darkness or exhaustion sets in.**

the siting of a shelter and the form it takes. But there are some general points worth keeping in mind when considering the task of building a shelter.

If possible, choose the site that provides the most natural cover from the wind that you can find. If no site offering such protection is available, angle the shelter so that its entrance or open side is always facing away from the wind. Oddly enough, a hillside is usually warmer than a valley floor, even though it may be windier. Build the shelter as near as possible to a supply of fresh water, to sources of building materials and, very important, firewood. Any spot that is in a forest and near a fast-flowing stream can provide a site for a desirable, if temporary, residence. In lowlands be aware of the danger of floods. On the coast keep the tides in mind. In mountainous areas make sure that your prospective site does not lie in the path of possible avalanches or rockfalls. If you are in a forest, look around for fallen trees, which may indicate that it is an area of shallow soil. If the wind can blow one shallowly rooted tree over, it could do the same to others near you. For the same reason, isolated single trees are best avoided. On the other hand, the branches of an isolated tree which has already fallen may well provide a ready-made framework for a sound shelter.

Tuck yourself into a fallen fir tree. It may be damp, but you can increase your comfort by building a fire.

# CONSTRUCTION MATERIALS

In survival situations where a ready-made natural shelter is not available, the shelter is usually constructed from a combination of materials possessed by the survivor and natural materials found at or near the site. Probably the most useful example of the former is any type of sheeting. A groundsheet, plastic sheeting and sacks, canvas and blankets can all be used to provide a windproof shelter. Among the most commonly used natural materials are:

Groundsheet

Sacks

**Turf** Turf can be used for constructing a shelter in very flat, open areas where trees and shrubs are scarce. Indeed in many countries it is still used as an effective roofing material.

**Foliage** With foliage it is possible to construct an excellent, long-lasting waterproof shelter. If it is available, use large-leafed foliage.

Turf

**Stones** Where the ground is too hard to dig a shelter, or foliage is in very short supply, it is usually possible, though more time-consuming, to build a good shelter with large, flattish stones.

Foliage

## TERRAIN AND SHELTERS

Different types of terrain provide different features and materials for use in creating a shelter. The most commonly encountered types of terrain and the materials they furnish are examined below.

Stones

# FOREST

In any forested area there may be large fallen logs to be used. A trough dug between such logs, covered with a roof of branches and foliage, provides a shelter which requires little effort to construct. A single log can be supplemented with a low earth wall or used as the basis of a small lean-to.

The lean-to frame is the most commonly used shelter pattern-probably because it is among the simplest. When setting up the frame, make sure that the roof slopes down into the prevailing wind. The covering can be provided by a wide range of materials, from foliage to plastic sheeting, from a groundsheet to panels from a wrecked vehicle or aircraft. Even blocks of turf can be used. A firm mud or turf layer, when placed on top of foliage, will harden, prevent the shelter cover from being blown away and make it more windproof and waterproof. The sides of the shelter can either be filled in by using a similar combination of foliage and mud or turf, or they can be built up with blocks of turf.

One of the best shelters to build is a simple lean-to. Note the wind direction and then site your frame accordingly, using available branches to construct it. Cover the frame with foliage thick enough to stop the wind and rain, and then cover the sides to give extra protection.

## LAYERED TREE BIVOUAC

A small bivouac-like shelter can be made quite quickly from any small tree. Cut partially through the trunk at about shoulder height until you are able to push the upper part over so that its top rests on the ground. Do not detach this upper portion from the lower. Cut away the branches on its underside and break the upstanding branches on the outside so that they hang down. Thatch the shelter using the foliage cut from the underside.

If the survivor has a supply of usable cord or string, a variation of the lean-to can be built that is especially suitable in any area covered with short, bushy vegetation. Cut four or five stakes of the greatest length available. Force their ends into the ground, then bend the tops over and tie them down at an angle of 45 degrees. It may be possible to find a spot where two or three can be incorporated into the framework of the shelter without being cut-that is, they can left rooted in the ground. This will ensure that the shelter has much greater stability.

## PARACHUTE TENT

If you are lucky enough to have a parachute it is a simple matter to fashion a bell-tent from it. Parachute material is wind-resistant, and shower-proof as long as it is not touched, but it does not offer protection against heavy rain. First remove all the valuable paracord rigging lines. Tie a good length of cord to the centre of the parachute canopy. Tie a suitable log or stone to the other end and lob the cord over a convenient tree branch. Pull the parachute to its full height and secure the cord to the trunk. It is then a simple matter of pulling out the parachute skirt and pegging it in a

circle. The tent can be improved by cutting one side of a panel to form a door-on the lee side. A stove suitable for use inside this kind of shelter is the Yukon stove.

Twigs and branches can be tightly interwoven to provide a firm, hard frame. More foliage is then added until a complete covering is formed. A layer of light turf or mud will complete the roof.

# PLAINS AND GRASSLANDS

If you find yourself in an area which is covered with grass but where trees are either scarce or completely absent, it is possible to cut turf bricks and build an effective shelter. Making the roof will be easiest if you can find any small sticks or boughs to support a turf roof. An alternative form of roof is any kind of sheeting which can be anchored by the top row of turf bricks. If nothing but turf is at hand, make the shelter small and narrow enough for longer turf strips to be used in pairs, supporting each other, for the walls.

If the grass is long enough, bundles might be suitable to make a thatched roof for the shelter, but in this case try to pitch the roof as near to 45 degrees as practicable to provide a run-off for any water.

If the ground is suitable-that is, soft but not wet-it may be possible to combine the effort of digging or cutting the turf with building a low wall along the edge of the slit trench produced in the process.

Before bricks, most houses were constructed with a timber frame supporting wattle and daub—a lattice-work of sticks caked with mud. The same method can be used to build shelters on plains and grasslands.

In areas of short bush, a willow shelter can be made by overlapping saplings to form a frame. This can be covered with a shelter sheet, plastic sacking or a parachute.

Turf blocks make a wet but windproof shelter. Insulate the ground as well as possible, since it will inevitably fill with a little water (below).

The effective height of the windbreak is then increased for about the same amount of effort. It is essential to make sure, however, that any rain will drain away from the trench and not into it.

Making a shelter below ground level can also be very helpful in hot conditions, although when the weather is hot the hardness of the ground frequently makes this difficult.

All these shelters, and especially the lean-to varieties, can be improved by the addition of a fire and fire reflector. The fire is best set on a base of green logs, while the reflector is made of interwoven green sticks. Large stones stacked around the back of the fire will also reflect heat. The hot stones can be taken into the shelter at night. With care these can be placed beneath your bed space, where they will continue to emit warmth during the night.

# SNOW

There are several types of shelter that are used specifically in snow-covered terrain. However, some of them suffer from significant drawbacks. One type may demand too much time and energy in its construction, especially for a solitary survivor. Another might require a greater depth of snow than is available. Alternatively, very cold, hard-packed snow may not be available for the cutting of snow blocks.

## SNOW TRENCH

Even a hole in the snow provides temporary shelter as an emergency measure, and it can be improved to make a simple shelter for one man. If the snow is soft, branches or sheeting will be needed for the roof.

> **SURVIVAL TIP**
> Constructing a snow hole requires a great deal of effort, but you can make it easier by removing the undergarments from the top half of your body and tunnelling into the snow with waterproofs covering both the top and bottom half. Put the dry under-garments back on when the hole is complete.

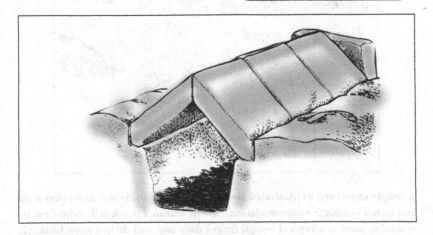

At the very least a snow trench will protect you from the wind. But with small refinements, such as pine branches for insulation, and a candle, it provides a good night's sleep.

## FIR-TREE SHELTER

If in a wooded snow-covered area, by far the most convenient and simplest shelter is to be found under a large fir tree. There will in many cases be a natural hollow in the snow around the trunk of the

A simple snow cave, as illustrated above, can be easily excavated and offers snug and secure overnight accommodation. (1) The entrance porch is dug out first, by removing snow in a vertical trough from a deep and well-drifted snow bank. (2) Continue digging out a T-shaped hole to a depth of about a metre (3ft). The upper part of this shape will form the sleeping area. (3) Carry on excavating the horizontal sleeping area a further metre (3ft) beyond the end of the vertical entrance. Any snow removed can be used to build up walls around the porch that will give added protection from the wind. (4) Cut snow blocks large enough to fill the front of the SURVIVAL SHELTERS sleeping area. (5) Leave gaps between the blocks for ventilation. (6) Crawl in and upwards onto the sleeping area. Dig upwards to create a domed roof and leave the entrance well open for further ventilation. If the wind is too strong the well can be closed with a rucksack.

tree and this will give you a good starting-point for building the shelter. First dig away the snow from the base of the tree and use it to build up and improve protection from the weather either side of the shelter. Cut the low branches on the side away from the shelter to use as bedding or to interweave with the branches on your side to improve the overhead cover. You can build a fire under the tree, but make sure it is at least part of the way around the trunk from your shelter, to stop it melting snow overhead.

## SNOW CAVE

This type of shelter requires a depth of snow of 2 metres (6.5 feet) or more, and so it is appropriate in very cold regions where the snow level builds up for long periods. The simplest approach is to dig into a snow drift or cornice. To improve the snow cave, aim to incorporate as many of the features shown in the cross-section above as you can. Make sure that the inside roof is always dome-shaped, or you will wake up in the morning with it on your head.

In snow-covered woods, large fir trees make an excellent natural hollow in the snow. This can be insulated from the ground by cutting away some of the lower branches, at the same time creating soft bedding. Always make your fire on the other side of the tree.

**A raised platform inside a snow shelter stops the coldest air-which sinks-from getting in. A second channel is needed for ventilation.**

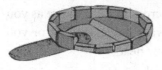

Igloo

Note that sometimes this type of shelter is considerably more difficult to make than it might seem, because of the hardness of the packed snow. In fact, without tools other than your hands and feet it may prove impossible.

### SNOW IGLOO

If the plan is to remain in one location for more than a day or two an igloo built of snow blocks will provide a good refuge for two or more survivors. It requires tools for its construction-an axe, a knife, and a saw or a spade. It also takes time and effort, as well as care and thought in placing the blocks. However, the combined efforts of two or three people will reduce the difficulty considerably.

**The secret of building a good igloo is to angle the lowest layer of blocks so that walls slope inward.**

The blocks must be cut from cold, heavily compacted snow-no other type of snow is suitable. Build up from the base, gradually working towards a point above the middle of the igloo, so that the blocks eventually join overhead.

An alternative method of constructing an igloo is to stamp down an area in the snow and build up a mound of packed snow, then simply tunnel into the mound. This method of construction has the advantage of being quick to construct, and is easier for the novice or the lone survivor.

Take care to lay out the entrance tunnel on the lee side of the shelter. In any snow shelter, build your bed on a raised platform, so as to avoid the coldest air, which will gather at the lowest level.

Where the snow is too shallow to build an igloo, a snow hive can be made.
(1) Pack snow on to a dome of branches covered with a sheet.
(2) Once the layer of snow is about 1ft (30cm) thick, carefully remove the branches and the sheet from the core.
(3) Use your rucksack or something similarly bulky to block up the entrance once you are inside the hive. Remember to leave a small gap in order to allow ventilation.
(4) This provides a surprisingly strong night shelter. On two occasions I have built hives and they can stand for seven days, so it is worth taking time to construct a large one.

**(1)** For survival shelter in longterm desert conditions, but where a building material is available, construct yourself a makeshift shelter by digging into a sand-dune.

**(2)** Sand has a habit of drifting and finding its way into every crevice. This can be minimized by using any wood and vehicle and aircraft parts you can find to form the basis of your shelter.

**(3)** The shelter should be covered, if at all possible, to protect you from the wind, sun and night-time cold—a real possibility under the cloudless skies of a desert.

As soon as you have constructed your igloo, place a lit candle in the centre. You will be surprised by the warmth generated by so little a fllame.

# DESERT AND ROCKY AREAS

The task of obtaining any form of shelter in desert areas presents several difficulties. However, the possibilities should be given some thought-not least because roughly one-fifth of the earth's surface falls into this category and survival situations frequently arise in such terrain.

The first difficulty is that deserts are places of extreme conditions-extreme heat during the day and biting cold at night. They also vary greatly in their composition, consisting of rock, sand or salt, or any combination of these. Some deserts are plains, others mountainous, still others depressions. Some are totally barren, others have scanty vegetation, while some have a variety of plants. All these variations can occur in combinations which make desert shelter difficult to achieve if you are entirely without material resource.

## THE SANGAR

A fortified combat position named after the Persian word for stone, a sangar is one of the earliest forms of man-made shelter. In the context of survival it is simply a windbreak built of any materials available-stones, branches, snow, parts from wrecked vehicle or aircraft, or indeed anything else that is suitable. In the absence of any better alternative, the sangar at least has the benefit of reducing exposure to the chilling effects of the wind. Use a survival blanket, poncho or plastic sheet as a roof to

A sangar is nothing more than a circle of stones. In the Middle East it provides protection against wild animals as well as the sun. An inner framework, supporting a sheet roof, much improves it.

**107**

If two forms of sheeting are available it is best to make a layered roof, leaving a 2–3in (5–7cm) gap. This allows air to circulate and drastically reduces the temperature.

**SURVIVAL TIP**

In jungle conditions there is usually an abundance of troublesome and unpleasant insects—on the ground. This means that a good basis for any shelter would be a raised platform. Even if your resources do not make it possible to build a platform big enough to support the entire shelter, it is very important to avoid sleeping directly on the jungle floor.

give shade by day and as a blanket at night, unless it is needed for protection against rain or snow.

Shelter from the sun and heat is the main aim when in the desert. Use a groundsheet (or any alternative) to cover a depression scooped out of the ground. This is known as a "scrape." If there are any rocks or vegetation, drape the sheet over the rocks or plants. If you have no material help, look for shade or shelter from natural desert features-rocks, rock cairns, caves or ledges. Dry stream beds may offer shelter. These wadi banks, or the sides of ravines or valleys, are worth looking over for crevices or caves.

## LONG-TERM DESERT SHELTER

Dig into the lee side of a dune, and make a roof from any material available. (A life-raft from a crashed aircraft is ideal. Use the paddles to support the inflated raft.) Cover the whole structure with any cloth or plastic material to prevent sand infiltrating it. If it is necessary, camouflage the whole shelter with sand, as this will not only aid concealment but will help to keep you cool during the day and warm during the night.

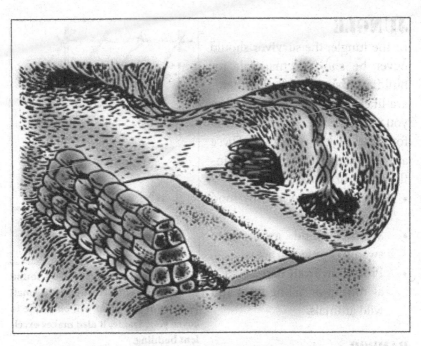

In mountainous desert areas, there is usually a good supply of caves. Always ensure that your selected cave is unoccupied. Form your fire at the deepest point and block the entrance against the wind and wild animals. Conditions can be made more tolerable by using soft sand from a valley floor to form a comfortable bed on rocky ground.

Whichever type of desert shelter you set out to build, remember that your aim is to protect yourself against those aspects of the environment which can threaten your safety. In any area with a hot climate, insects are likely to be a problem. You can gain some protection against the winged species if you are able to erect your shelter on a site which receives some breeze—for example, on a hillside or ridge, or in a location which receives an onshore wind.

> **SURVIVAL TIP**
> The jungle survivor must learn to work with the jungle, and not fight against it. And remember that, when you are wet, cold and perhaps miserable, every hour spent building your shelter and your fire is worth many hours' sleep.

# JUNGLE

In the jungle, the survivor should never be short of materials for building a shelter. All such items are likely to be close at hand, but you would do well to select the site for your shelter with care. These are the main factors that will influence your choice:

- The presence of nearby food and water.
- Stable ground away from swamp or infected areas.
- Protection from danger, such as rotting or falling trees and wild animals.

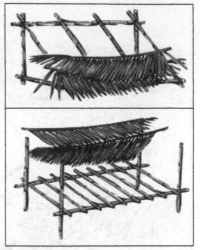

Foliage for shelters is easily found in any jungle. Normally just a small portion of one plant will be ample to cover your frame; it also makes excellent bedding.

## BAMBOO

Bamboo (atap) is one of the most commonly used building materials in survival in the jungle, but gathering it can be hazardous. Care should be taken when cutting bamboo as it grows very densely and in some growths sections are under strain. It is not uncommon for a cut section to suddenly shoot forward and hit you with some force. Bear in mind as well that bamboo is very sharp.

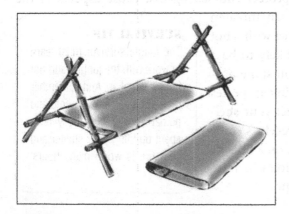

An A-frame pole bed is usually supported by two larger trees. The tension in the bed—which can be made from plastic feed sacks—holds the bedding poles in place.

Despite these drawbacks, bamboo is a wonderful material and with the aid of a good jungle knife, you can construct many useful survival items, including the shelter itself, a pole bed, cooking and drinking utensils, and even a serviceable raft. Vines are normally plentiful and only require pulling down from their branches, but again care should be exercised. Always look up first.

## POLE BED

Build your bed first and then construct your shelter over it. A pole bed of bamboo or any small branches covered with palm leaves or other foliage is a real necessity. If any sizeable suitable material is available then you should use that for the base.

## HAMMOCK

You can make a hammock if you have a parachute, since this will provide almost the ideal materials. However, do not attempt to make one out of vines since they normally break.

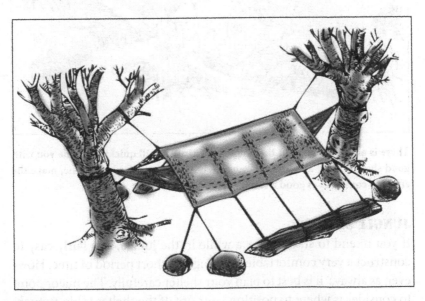

A perfect combination for a shelter in a warm climate is either a bed or hammock slung beneath a poncho or shelter sheet. Providing it does not become too cold, it is possible to live comfortably for many months underneath such an arrangement.

There is an old saying that the jungle is neutral. It will quickly provide you with good shelter, food, and water. If you intend to stay put for some time, make the effort to construct as good a camp as you can.

## JUNGLE SHELTER

If you intend to stay put for a while in the jungle, it is fairly easy to construct a very comfortable dwelling in a short period of time. However, as always, it is best to plan your shelter carefully. The major point to consider is where to position your fire. If the shelter is big enough, and there is no possibility of it catching fire, then inside is best. During the day the fire can be used for its normal functions, notably cooking,

Almost the biggest menace when you are in the jungle is not large animals, but insects. It is essential to sleep on a raised platform. Burning a termite nest keeps flies at bay—but the smoke can be almost as irritating. A layer of mud stops biting insects and can be washed off in the morning.

Use broad leaves to cover a jungle shelter. Large branches can be split and woven into a frame of saplings. Experiment with whatever cover is available in the vicinity.

while at dusk and during the night it can be used to fend off insects. A good idea is to burn a termites' nest if you can find one, since this will produce a great quantity of smoke which will keep the flying bugs away. However, bear in mind that it is not always clear which is the most evil of the two: the smoke or the mosquitoes. Spreading old ash around your bedding area and the shelter site will also help reduce the amount of crawling companions that gather during the night.

**113**

## CHAPTER 11

# SURVIVAL KITS

Survival kits must be matched to the environment in which you are most likely to find yourself. A home survival kit can easily contain power generators, fuel and food for weeks, robust medical supplies, communications equipment, and large quantities of water. When you are headed into a wilderness area or have the potential to be stranded in such an area, you will have to choose your items with more discretion and design a kit that you can carry for prolonged periods that will still provide you with those items you decide are critical to your survival.

From the previous chapters you should already have an idea of what items are most critical to any survival situation, such as a knife, map, compass, and items for making a fire. While many people quickly think of a firearm, you will note that scant attention has been given to that item. Remember that a basic tenant of any survival kit is selecting items that are multipurpose. Firearms are only good for killing game and signaling. Their cost is in their bulk and weight. In turn, a knife and hatchet or small ax will serve many purposes and not be dependant on ammunition. If you feel it is essential to have a firearm, choose one that is lightweight and uses light ammunition such as .22 cal, which will allow you to carry more rounds for the same weight and is fully sufficient for small game. Remember that small animals are more plentiful than large ones and dangerous animals should be avoided all together.

While the list of items you might include in your survival kit is huge and in many cases depends on personal preference, recommended kits for cold climates, hot climates, and water survival are listed below. These recommended kits are followed by a larger listing of items that you may consider for your own survival kit. While these recommended items in no way provide a comprehensive list of the items you can choose from, they do provide a basis from which you can select items for a basic kit.

| | |
|---|---|
| • Food packets | • Illuminating candles |
| • Snare wire | • Compressed trioxane fuel |
| • Illumination flares | • Signaling mirror |
| • Waterproof match box | • Survival fishing kit |
| • Saw/knife blade | • Plastic spoon |
| • Wood matches | • Survival manual |
| • First aid kit | • Poncho |
| • Magnetic compass | • Insect headnet |
| • Pocket knife | • Shovel |
| • Saw-knife-shovel handle | • Water bag |
| • Frying pan | • Sleeping bag |

**Cold Climate Kit**

| | |
|---|---|
| • Canned drinking water | • Compressed trioxane fuel |
| • Waterproof matchbox | • Fishing tackle kit |
| • Plastic whistle | • Magnetic compass |
| • Illumination flares | • Snare wire |
| • Pocket knife | • Frying pan |
| • Signaling mirror | • Wood matches |
| • Plastic water bag | • Insect headnet |
| • First aid kit | • Reversible sun hat |
| • Sunburn-preventive cream | • Tarpaulin |
| • Plastic spoon | • Survival manual |
| • Food packets | |

**Hot Climate Kit**

- Raft boat paddle
- Survival manual
- Insect headnet
- Reversible sun hat
- Water storage bag
- Magnetic compass
- Boat bailer
- Sponge
- Sunburn-preventive cream
- Wood matches
- First aid kit
- Plastic spoon

- Plastic knife
- Food packets
- Fluorescent sea marker
- Frying pan
- Seawater desalter kit
- Compressed trioxane fuel
- Illumination flares
- Signaling mirror
- Fishing tackle box
- Waterproof match box
- Raft repair kit

**Overwater Kit**

- Hunting knife with a 5-in. blade, leather handle, and sheath
- Pocket knife with one 3-1/16 in. lg cutting blade, & one 1-25/32 in. lg hook blade, w/safety lock & clevis
- Emergency signaling mirror
- Signal kit, with flares or rocket launcher
- Medical kit in a self contained carrying bag with insect repellent & sun screen ointment
- 1 bar soap,
- Adhesive tape surgical
- Aspirin tablets
- Band-Aids
- Bandage gauze, elastic: white, sterile, 2 in. w, 180 in. lg
- Disinfectant ointment
- Water purification tablets, or filtration device
- Plastic whistle, ball

**Other Items**

## CHAPTER 12

# EDIBLE/MEDICINAL PLANTS

In a survival situation, plants can provide food and medicine. Their safe usage requires absolutely positive identification, knowing how to prepare them for eating, and knowing any dangerous properties they might have. Familiarity with botanical structures of plants and information on where they grow will make them easier to locate and identify.

## AGAVE

*Agave* species

**DESCRIPTION:** These plants have large clusters of thick, fleshy leaves borne close to the ground and surrounding a central stalk. The plants flower only once, then die. They produce a massive flower stalk.

**HABITAT AND DISTRIBUTION:** Agaves prefer dry, open areas. They are found throughout Central America, the Caribbean, and parts of the western deserts of the United States and Mexico.

**EDIBLE PARTS:** Its flowers and flower buds are edible. Boil them before eating.

## CAUTION

The juice of some species causes dermatitis in some individuals.

**OTHER USES:** Cut the huge flower stalk and collect the juice for drinking. Some species have very fibrous leaves. Pound the leaves and remove the fibers for weaving and making ropes. Most species have thick, sharp needles at the tips of the leaves. Use them for sewing or making hacks. The sap of some species contains a chemical that makes the sap suitable for use as a soap.

# ARROWROOT

*Maranta* and *Sagittaria* species

**DESCRIPTION:** The arrowroot is an aquatic plant with arrow-shaped leaves and potato-like tubers in the mud.

**HABITAT AND DISTRIBUTION:** Arrowroot is found worldwide in temperate zones and the tropics. It is found in moist to wet habitats.

**EDIBLE PARTS:** The rootstock is a rich source of high quality starch. Boil the rootstock and eat it as a vegetable.

COURTESY OF WIBOWO DJATMIKO

# BAMBOO

Various species including *Bambusa, Dendrocalamus, Phyllostachys*

**DESCRIPTION:** Bamboos are woody grasses that grow up to 15 meters tall. The leaves are grass-like and the stems are the familiar bamboo used in furniture and fishing poles.

**HABITAT AND DISTRIBUTION:** Look for bamboo in warm, moist regions in open or jungle country, in lowland, or on mountains. Bamboos are native to the Far East (Temperate and Tropical zones) but have been widely planted around the world.

**EDIBLE PARTS:** The young shoots of almost all species are edible raw or cooked. Raw shoots have a slightly bitter taste that is removed by boiling. To prepare, remove the tough protective sheath that is coated with tawny or red hairs. The seed grain of the flowering bamboo is also edible. Boil the seeds like rice or pulverize them, mix with water, and make into cakes.

**OTHER USES:** Use the mature bamboo to build structures or to make containers, ladles, spoons, and various other cooking utensils. Also use bamboo to make tools and weapons. You can make a strong bow by splitting the bamboo and putting several pieces together.

## CAUTION

Green bamboo may explode in a fire. Green bamboo has an internal membrane you must remove before using it as a food or water container.

# BBLACKBERRY, RASPBERRY, AND DEW-BERRY

*Rubus* species

**DESCRIPTION:** These plants have prickly stems (canes) that grow upward, arching back toward the ground. They have alternate, usually compound leaves. Their fruits may be red, black, yellow, or orange.

**HABITAT AND DISTRIBUTION:** These plants grow in open, sunny areas at the margin of woods, lakes, streams, and roads throughout temperate regions. There is also an arctic raspberry.

**EDIBLE PARTS:** The fruits and peeled young shoots are edible. Flavor varies greatly.

**OTHER USES:** Use the leaves to make tea. To treat diarrhea, drink a tea made by brewing the dried root bark of the blackberry bush.

# BLUEBERRY AND HUCKLEBERRY

*Vaccinium* and *Gaylussacia* species

**DESCRIPTION:** These shrubs vary in size from 30 centimeters to 3.7 meters tall. All have alternate, simple leaves. Their fruits may be dark blue, black, or red and have many small seeds.

**HABITAT AND DISTRIBUTION:** These plants prefer open, sunny areas. They are found throughout much of the north temperate regions and at higher elevations in Central America.

**EDIBLE PARTS:** Their fruits are edible raw.

# CATTAIL

*Typha latifolia*

---

**DESCRIPTION:** Cattails are grass-like plants with strap-shaped leaves 1 to 5 centimeters wide and growing up to 1.8 meters tall. The male flowers are borne in a dense mass above the female flowers. These last only a short time, leaving the female flowers that develop into the brown cattail. Pollen from the male flowers is often abundant and bright yellow.

**HABITAT AND DISTRIBUTION:** Cattails are found throughout most of the world. Look for them in full sun areas at the margins of lakes, streams, canals, rivers, and brackish water.

**EDIBLE PARTS:** The young tender shoots are edible raw or cooked. The rhizome is often very tough but is a rich source of starch. Pound the rhizome to remove the starch and use as a flour. The pollen is also an exceptional source of starch. When the cattail is immature and still green, you can boil the female portion and eat it like corn on the cob.

**OTHER USES:** The dried leaves are an excellent source of weaving material you can use to make floats and rafts. The cottony seeds make good pillow stuffing and insulation. The fluff makes excellent tinder. Dried cattails are effective insect repellents when burned.

# CHICORY

*Cichorium intybus*

**DESCRIPTION:** This plant grows up to 1.8 meters tall. It has leaves clustered at the base of the stem and some leaves on the stem. The base leaves resemble those of the dandelion. The flowers are sky blue and stay open only on sunny days. Chicory has a milky juice.

**HABITAT AND DISTRIBUTION:** Look for chicory in old fields, waste areas, weedy lots, and along roads. It is a native of Europe and Asia, but is also found in Africa and most of North America where it grows as a weed.

**EDIBLE PARTS:** All parts are edible. Eat the young leaves as a salad or boil to eat as a vegetable. Cook the roots as a vegetable. For use as a coffee substitute, roast the roots until they are dark brown and then pulverize them.

# CHUFA

*Cyperus esculentus*

**DESCRIPTION:** This very common plant has a triangular stem and grass-like leaves. It grows to a height of 20 to 60 centimeters. The mature plant has a soft fur-like bloom that extends from a whorl of leaves. Tubers 1 to 2.5 centimeters in diameter grow at the ends of the roots.

**HABITAT AND DISTRIBUTION:** Chufa grows in moist sandy areas throughout the world. It is often an abundant weed in cultivated fields.

**EDIBLE PARTS:** The tubers are edible raw, boiled, or baked. You can also grind them and use them as a coffee substitute.

COURTESY OF STANLEY KAYS

# CRANBERRY

*Vaccinium macrocarpon*

**DESCRIPTION:** This plant has tiny leaves arranged alternately. Its stem creeps along the ground. Its fruits are red berries.

**HABITAT AND DISTRIBUTION:** It only grows in open, sunny, wet areas in the colder regions of the Northern Hemisphere.

**EDIBLE PARTS:** The berries are very tart when eaten raw. Cook in a small amount of water and add sugar, if available, to make a jelly.

**OTHER USES:** Cranberries may act as a diuretic. They are useful for treating urinary tract infections.

# CROWBERRY

*Empetrum nigrum*

**DESCRIPTION:** This is a dwarf evergreen shrub with short needlelike leaves. It has small, shiny, black berries that remain on the bush throughout the winter.

**HABITAT AND DISTRIBUTION:** Look for this plant in tundra throughout arctic regions of North America and Eurasia.

**EDIBLE PARTS:** The fruits are edible fresh or can be dried for later use.

# DATE PALM

*Phoenix dactylifera*

**DESCRIPTION:** The date palm is a tall, unbranched tree with a crown of huge, compound leaves. Its fruit is yellow when ripe.

**HABITAT AND DISTRIBUTION:** This tree grows in arid semitropical regions. It is native to North Africa and the Middle East but has been planted in the arid semitropics in other parts of the world.

**EDIBLE PARTS:** Its fruit is edible fresh but is very bitter if eaten before it is ripe. You can dry the fruits in the sun and preserve them for a long time.

**OTHER USES:** The trunks provide valuable building material in desert regions where few other treelike plants are found. The leaves are durable and you can use them for thatching and as weaving material. The base of the leaves resembles coarse cloth that you can use for scrubbing and cleaning.

# FIREWEED

*Epilobium angustifolium*

---

**DESCRIPTION:** This plant grows up to 1.8 meters tall. It has large, showy, pink flowers and lance-shaped leaves. Its relative, the dwarf fireweed (*Epilobium latifolium*), grows 30 to 60 centimeters tall.

**HABITAT AND DISTRIBUTION:** Tall fireweed is found in open woods, on hillsides, on stream banks, and near seashores in arctic regions. It is especially abundant in burned-over areas. Dwarf fireweed is found along streams, sandbars, and lakeshores and on alpine and arctic slopes.

**EDIBLE PARTS:** The leaves, stems, and flowers are edible in the spring but become tough in summer. You can split open the stems of old plants and eat the pith raw.

COURTESY OF A. BARRA

# HACKBERRY

*Celtis* species

---

**DESCRIPTION:** Hackberry trees have smooth, gray bark that often has corky warts or ridges. The tree may reach 39 meters in height. Hackberry trees have long-pointed leaves that grow in two rows. This tree bears small, round berries that can be eaten when they are ripe and fall from the tree. The wood of the hackberry is yellowish.

**HABITAT AND DISTRIBUTION:** This plant is widespread in the United States, especially in and near ponds.

**EDIBLE PARTS:** Its berries are edible when they are ripe and fall from the tree.

# JUNIPER

*Juniperus* species

---

**DESCRIPTION:** Junipers, sometimes called cedars, are trees or shrubs with very small, scale-like leaves densely crowded around the branches. Each leaf is less than 1.2 centimeters long. All species have a distinct aroma resembling the well-known cedar. The berrylike cones are usually blue and covered with a whitish wax.

**HABITAT AND DISTRIBUTION:** Look for junipers in open, dry, sunny areas throughout North America and northern Europe. Some species are found in southeastern Europe, across Asia to Japan, and in the mountains of North Africa.

**EDIBLE PARTS:** The berries and twigs are edible. Eat the berries raw or roast the seeds to use as a coffee substitute. Use dried and crushed berries as a seasoning for meat. Gather young twigs to make a tea.

## CAUTION

Many plants may be called cedars but are not related to junipers and may be harmful. Always look for the berrylike structures, needle leaves, and resinous, fragrant sap to be sure the plant you have is a juniper.

# MARSH MARIGOLD

*Caltha palustris*

---

**DESCRIPTION:** This plant has rounded, dark green leaves arising from a short stem. It has bright yellow flowers.

**HABITAT AND DISTRIBUTION:** This plant is found in bogs, lakes, and slow-moving streams. It is abundant in arctic and subarctic regions and in much of the eastern region of the northern United States.

**EDIBLE PARTS:** All parts are edible if boiled.

## CAUTION

As with all water plants, do not eat this plant raw. Raw water plants may carry dangerous organisms that are removed only by cooking.

# NETTLE

*Urtica* and *Laportea* species

**DESCRIPTION:** These plants grow several feet high. They have small, inconspicuous flowers. Fine, hair-like bristles cover the stems, leafstalks, and undersides of leaves. The bristles cause a stinging sensation when they touch the skin.

**HABITAT AND DISTRIBUTION:** Nettles prefer moist areas along streams or at the margins of forests. They are found throughout North America, Central America, the Caribbean, and northern Europe.

**EDIBLE PARTS:** Young shoots and leaves are edible. Boiling the plant for 10 to 15 minutes destroys the stinging element of the bristles. This plant is very nutritious.

**OTHER USES:** Mature stems have a fibrous layer that can be divided into individual fibers and used to weave string or twine.

# OAK

*Quercus* species

**DESCRIPTION:** Oak trees have alternate leaves and acorn fruits. There are two main groups of oaks: red and white. The red oak group has leaves with bristles and smooth bark in the upper part of the tree. Red oak acorns take 2 years to mature. The white oak group has leaves without bristles and a rough bark in the upper portion of the tree. White oak acorns mature in 1 year.

**HABITAT AND DISTRIBUTION:** Oak trees are found in many habitats throughout North America, Central America, and parts of Europe and Asia.

**EDIBLE PARTS:** All parts are edible, but often contain large quantities of bitter substances. White oak acorns usually have a better flavor than red oak acorns. Gather and shell the acorns. Soak red oak acorns in water for 1 to 2 days to remove the bitter substance. You can speed up this process by putting wood ashes in the water in which you soak the acorns. Boil the acorns or grind them into flour and use the flour for baking. You can use acorns that you baked until very dark as a coffee substitute.

## CAUTION

Tannic acid gives the acorns their bitter taste. Eating an excessive amount of acorns high in tannic acid can lead to kidney failure. Before eating acorns, leach out this chemical.

**OTHER USES:** Oak wood is excellent for building or burning. Small oaks can be split and cut into long thin strips (3 to 6 millimeters thick and 1.2 centimeters wide) used to weave mats, baskets, or frameworks for packs, sleds, furniture, etc. Oak bark soaked in water produces a tanning solution used to preserve leather.

# PALMETTO PALM

*Sabal palmetto*

**DESCRIPTION:** The palmetto palm is a tall, unbranched tree with persistent leaf bases on most of the trunk. The leaves are large, simple, and palmately lobed. Its fruits are dark blue or black with a hard seed.

**HABITAT AND DISTRIBUTION:** The palmetto palm is found throughout the coastal regions of the southeastern United States.

**EDIBLE PARTS:** The fruits are edible raw. The hard seeds may be ground into flour. The heart of the palm is a nutritious food source at any time. Cut off the top of the tree to obtain the palm heart.

**133**

# PURSLANE

*Portulaca oleracea*

---

**DESCRIPTION:** This plant grows close to the ground. It is seldom more than a few centimeters tall. Its stems and leaves are fleshy and often tinged with red. It has paddle-shaped leaves, 2.5 centimeters or less long, clustered at the tips of the stems. Its flowers are yellow or pink. Its seeds are tiny and black.

**HABITAT AND DISTRIBUTION:** It grows in full sun in cultivated fields, field margins, and other weedy areas throughout the world.

**EDIBLE PARTS:** All parts are edible. Wash and boil the plants for a tasty vegetable or eat them raw. Use the seeds as a flour substitute or eat them raw.

# REED

*Phragmites australis*

**DESCRIPTION:** This tall, coarse grass grows to 3.5 meters tall and has gray-green leaves about 4 centimeters wide. It has large masses of brown flower branches in early summer. These rarely produce grain and become fluffy, gray masses late in the season.

**HABITAT AND DISTRIBUTION:** Look for reed in any open, wet area, especially one that has been disturbed through dredging. Reed is found throughout the temperate regions of both the Northern and Southern Hemispheres.

**EDIBLE PARTS:** All parts of the plant are edible raw or cooked in any season. Harvest the stems as they emerge from the soil and boil them. You can also harvest them just before they produce flowers, then dry and beat them into flour. You can also dig up and boil the underground stems, but they are often tough. Seeds are edible raw or boiled, but they are rarely found.

# SORGHUM

*Sorghum* species

**DESCRIPTION:** There are many different kinds of sorghum, all of which bear grains in heads at the top of the plants. The grains are brown, white, red, or black. Sorghum is the main food crop in many parts of the world.

**HABITAT AND DISTRIBUTION:** Sorghum is found worldwide, usually in warmer climates. All species are found in open, sunny areas.

**EDIBLE PARTS:** The grains are edible at any stage of development. When young, the grains are milky and edible raw. Boil the older grains. Sorghum is a nutritious food.

**OTHER USES:** Use the stems of tall sorghum as building materials.

# WATER LILY

*Nymphaea odorata*

**DESCRIPTION:** These plants have large, triangular leaves that float on the water's surface, large, fragrant flowers that are usually white, or red, and thick, fleshy rhizomes that grow in the mud.

**HABITAT AND DISTRIBUTION:** Water lilies are found throughout much of the temperate and subtropical regions.

**EDIBLE PARTS:** The flowers, seeds, and rhizomes are edible raw or cooked. To prepare rhizomes for eating, peel off the corky rind. Eat raw, or slice thinly, allow to dry, and then grind into flour. Dry, parch, and grind the seeds into flour.

**OTHER USES:** Use the liquid resulting from boiling the thickened root in water as a medicine for diarrhea and as a gargle for sore throats.

# WATER LILY